# WOODBINE WILLIE

*To Annette – The Best*

# WOODBINE WILLIE
## An Unsung Hero of World War One

## BOB HOLMAN

LION

Published by Lion Books
an imprint of
**Lion Hudson plc**
Wilkinson House, Jordan Hill Road,
Oxford OX2 8DR, England
www.lionhudson.com/lion

ISBN 978 0 7459 5561 2
e-ISBN 978 0 7459 5713 5

First edition 2013

**Acknowledgments**
pp. 40, 43, 47, 87, 98, 101, 105, 155, 168, 170: From *After War, Is Faith
Possible? G. A. Studdert Kennedy, "Woodbine Willie." An Anthology* copyright ©
2008 edited by Kerry Walters. Reprinted by permission of The Lutterworth
Press.
pp. 23, 28, 120, 124, 138, 157, 166, 167: From "The Way of Life", BBC radio
programme broadcast in 1962. Reprinted by permission of the BBC.
pp. 11, 38, 42, 69, 70, 71, 174: From *The Church of England and the First World
War* © 1978 by Alan Wilkinson. Reprinted by permission of SPCK.
pp. 13–14, 27, 29, 62, 82, 95, 126–27, 139, 153, 157, 158, 167, 169: From
*A Fiery Glow in the Darkness: Woodbine Willie, Padre and Poet* © 1997 by
Michael Grundy. Reprinted by permission of Osborne Books Ltd.
pp. 179–80: From Where is God Amidst the Bombs? © 2008 by Neal
Goldsborough. Reprinted by permission of Neal Goldsborough

A catalogue record for this book is available from the British Library

Printed and bound in Great Britain, February 2013, LH26

# CONTENTS

# Introduction

The year 1953 was memorable: the coronation of Queen Elizabeth, a British team climbed Mount Everest, and Stanley Matthews finally won a cup winner's medal at Wembley. For me, a seventeen-year-old in Ilford, it was memorable for another reason. Mr Jack Jenkins, a deacon at the Baptist church I attended, gave me a book entitled *The Unutterable Beauty: The Collected Poetry of G. A. Studdert Kennedy*. First published in 1927, it was frequently reprinted. I am still fascinated by Geoffrey Anketell Studdert Kennedy, often known as Woodbine Willie, who was a chaplain in the First World War and then an outstanding priest, preacher, and advocate for social reform. I was delighted when Lion Hudson asked me to write his biography.

A number of people have contributed to this book. Canon Paul Tongue, whose father was a member of Studdert Kennedy's church in Worcester, has shared his extensive knowledge with me. The Reverend Andrew Studdert-Kennedy is a grandson who, in an interview, gave me many insights. One of his sons, Professor Michael Studdert-Kennedy, took the trouble to communicate with me by email from the USA. Another grandson, Nigel Studdert-Kennedy, also gave me helpful information.

David Morrison, at the Worcester Cathedral Archives, kindly and diligently introduced me to papers, letters, and articles about Studdert Kennedy. William Cole, who now works at St Edmund's Church in London, where Studdert Kennedy was rector for a period, has given me his time and introduced me to a brilliant but forgotten portrait of him. My friend Gary Boon, who works for the BBC, has tracked down broadcasts about Studdert Kennedy and, with his daughter Joanna, has been a source of encouragement. Another good friend, Mick Popplewell, has sought out original information about the background of Emily Catlow, who became the wife of Studdert Kennedy. The writings of Michael Grundy, Alan Wilkinson, and William Purcell have been essential. Above all, my wife Annette has, as always, taken a great interest in what I am writing and has freed me from household and gardening tasks.

Not least, my thanks to my commissioning editor at Lion Hudson, Ali Hull, who has given me sound and wise advice.

Lastly, my grandsons Lucas and Nathan keep me even more occupied than the book. But the happiness I gain from their company gives me pleasure that I would not sacrifice for a hundred books.

**Bob Holman**

# 1

## Childhood and Education, 1883–1904

*It was a common enough scene in those days, an advanced collecting post for wounded in the Ypres Salient, on the evening of June 15, 1917. Twenty men all smashed up and crammed together in a little concrete shelter which would have been full with ten in it. Outside the German barrage banging down all round us… A boy with a badly shattered thigh in a corner moaning and yelling by turns for "Somefing to stop the pain." So it had been for an hour or more. Between this Black Hole of Calcutta and Battalion H.Q. Death and Hell to go through. Hell inside and Hell out, and the moaning of the boy in the corner like the moaning of a damned soul.*

*There was no morphine. That was the horror. Someone must go for it. I went. I went because the hell outside was less awful than the hell in. I didn't go to do an heroic deed or perform a Christian service; I went because I couldn't bear the moaning any longer. I ran, and as I ran, and cowered down in shell-holes waiting for a chance to run again, I thought – thought like lightning – whole trains of thought came tearing through my mind like non-stop expresses to God knows where. I thought: Poor devil, I couldn't have stood that a minute longer. I wasn't doing any good either. If I get through and bring the morphia back, it will be like bringing heaven to him. That is the only heaven he wants just now, dead-drunk sleep. If I bring it back I will be to him a saviour from hell. I'd like that. I'm glad I thought of that. I can't pretend that it was that I came for. It wasn't. Still I'm glad. He wants to forget, to forget and sleep. Poor old chap. Heaven is a morphia pill.[1]*

8

The writer of these words did get through the shells and bullets. The wounded got the morphine, and the writer was awarded the Military Cross. His name was Geoffrey Studdert Kennedy, although he was nicknamed "Woodbine Willie" because of his habit of doling out cigarettes to the troops.

These troops who lived in the trenches and survived the First World War did not just remember the fighting. Some could always smell the stink of buckets used as toilets. Others always shuddered at the thought of thousands of rats who chewed anything, including dead bodies, and licked the sweat off the faces of sleeping men. For some it was the freezing cold which, on guard duty, was so intense that they lost movement in their legs. For Studdert Kennedy it was the screams of wounded soldiers, particularly as he dragged them from the front line to the hospital.

Geoffrey Studdert Kennedy was a Church of England priest who in 1916, at the age of thirty-three, had volunteered to be a chaplain. Very quickly he was on the front line, helping doctors treat the injured, trying to staunch the blood, holding them during operations, and offering words of hope. Frequently he advanced with the men when they went over the top towards enemy fire. He would drag back the badly wounded, pray over the dying, and bury the dead. He was sometimes described as ugly. He might have lacked good looks but he never lacked courage.

## His Childhood

Geoffrey Anketell Studdert Kennedy was born in a vicarage in Leeds on 27 June 1883. He was thus a Victorian, part of a Britain noted for its industrial wealth and worldwide empire. But there was another side of Britain – people in poverty. At this time, studies of poverty were few. One of the first was Seebohm Rowntree's survey of York, for which he interviewed a large sample of people and took precise measurements of their incomes and expenditures.[2] In 2007, Gazeley and Newell used newly discovered material from 1904 which had been based on the Rowntree approach. They revealed that in northern towns such as Leeds, some 16.8 per cent of the wage-earning class was in primary poverty; that is, their income was not sufficient to meet "the necessities of life". For a couple with three children this meant their weekly income was below 21s. 8d. a week.[3] The area of Quarry Hill, where Studdert Kennedy was born, was characterized by back-to-back housing with the grim workhouse, the Cemetery Tavern, and the parish church of St Mary's in the midst.

Geoffrey Studdert Kennedy's father, the Reverend William Studdert Kennedy, was the vicar of St Mary's. Born in 1826, he was an Irishman and the son of a clergyman. He served at churches in Ballymena and Dublin before moving to a church in Forton, Lancashire, and then to St Mary's. With his first wife, a Miss Russell from Malahide in Ireland, he had five children, named Mabel, Norah, Eve, Frances, and John Russell. After the death of this wife, the Reverend William married nineteen-year-old Joan Anketell, also from Ireland, by whom he had a further nine children who were, according to age, Rachel, Kathleen, William, Robert, Hugh, Maurice, Geoffrey, Cecil, and Gerald. The family was large even by Victorian standards and included William's mother for a while.

Of the seven boys, four were ordained into the ministry. Most of Geoffrey's siblings were academically able, with two taking degrees at Trinity College, Dublin, and they no doubt stimulated his own educational progress. He kept in touch with his siblings as they all grew up, and some of them left affectionate records of him and his childhood, including his brother William. Commenting on Geoffrey's early years, William wrote:

> *Mother always said he was the best baby she ever had. When he was about two years old (or less) a storm one night blew down a chimney, and some bricks fell through the ceiling close to his cot. I remember him being carried down into the nursery – and his chubby face and big smile. His first attack of asthma was when he was about six or seven. I can see him now with his large eyes, languidly playing with a wooden horse, and enduring my clumsy efforts to entertain him. He*

*always had an extraordinary laugh, which would have been unpleasant but for the fact that it was so perfectly real.*[4]

In turn, Maurice wrote:

*One thing that impressed itself considerably on me in regard to him at every stage of his life was his gentle, forgiving, loving nature. He would blaze with indignation at anything nasty, mean, unmanly, treacherous or unkind – any wrong or injustice done to another; but always took with a good natured smile – or with a patient sad forgiveness – any injustice to himself.*[5]

He added, "There were lots of good natured family jokes at his expense – particularly in regard to his capacity for becoming entirely lost and absorbed in every sort of book."[6]

His sister, Rachel, commented:

*He was always very fond of reading, and even before he could read himself would sit still as long as anyone would read to him. His first lessons were of rather a spasmodic nature: first one elder sister or brother would take him in hand for a while and then another, but he managed to glean a good deal of information for himself, for even as a child he was a thinker. On one well remembered occasion, when disappointed that he could not do something that he had been promised for a long time, he declared with great conviction, "everything has a beginning and everything has an end" – evidently thinking that some day he would be able to do as the others did. Sometimes his absent mindedness got him into difficulties; sent with a message, one was never quite certain what would happen; there is a family tradition that Geoff was once sent to the greengrocer's to order two pounds of strawberries and a stone of potatoes; the man delivered two stones of strawberries and two pounds of potatoes.*[7]

These loving commendations all came from siblings but Geoffrey does come over as a loving and kindly young man.

Joan Studdert Kennedy was an exceptional woman. The census records show that some of the children from the first marriage still lived with the family at various times. John Russell was there for a while and, in 1901, so were Mabel, Norah, and Eve, although they were all over thirty and may well have made practical and financial contributions to the home. The census of 1881 also shows a cook in residence and the census of 1901 mentions a nurse. But it was Joan who oversaw the running of the home and ensured that harmony was maintained. She also cared for her husband, managed the large vicarage, helped in parish work, and participated in a secular choir in Leeds – perhaps that was her relaxation. Clearly she was a woman who was devoted to her family, and Geoffrey later displayed a similar characteristic.

Remembering his mother in later years, Geoffrey wrote:

> *When I was a very small boy, I was called with my brothers into my mother's room on a Sunday afternoon to have what were called Scripture lessons… The real interest of the lessons began for me when my mother produced an old book with brown battered covers and began to read – with a soft Irish brogue – the immortal prose of Pilgrim's Progress.*[8]

Little is recorded of how his father related individually to Geoffrey. He led a busy life with so many children and a large parish, so his time must have been limited. But it is clear that he participated joyfully in family gatherings, debates, and celebrations. Geoffrey's best friend from secondary school, J. K. Mozley, who later became an Anglican minister and well-known writer, spent much of his time at the Studdert Kennedy home. He recalled that he never had to knock on the door but just walked in and always received a warm welcome from the family and then enjoyed "the deep harmony which prevailed among them".[9] Brother Gerald especially treasured Christmas at the home and wrote:

*Christmas at St Mary's Vicarage was a time of uproarious laughter. Ghost stories and detective stories all mixed up together with deep and prolonged discussions about theology, psychology, metaphysics, economics, ethics, evolution, etc., prolonged until well after midnight. In all which, as may easily be imagined, Geoffrey was a protagonist. I well remember father turning to me one day after a very brain-cracking discussion, and saying with a chuckle: "When I discuss things with dear Geoff, I almost see the perspiration coming out the top of his head, his brain seems to be working so hard."*[10]

The Church of England has had many unknown clergy who devoted their lives to serving their parishioners. The Reverend William Studdert Kennedy was one such, a priest who would now be almost forgotten had he not been the father of Geoffrey. His church was a very large building which was rarely filled to capacity. He worked hard and diligently, never seeking and never gaining distinction. Years later, Geoffrey observed that his father did not win many to Christianity but those he did tended to stay faithful for life.

J. K. Mozley noticed from his stays at the vicarage that "The district was very poor... When I first knew it, before large measures of slum clearance was carried out, it was, especially near the church, a region of poor and ill-lighted streets and alleys."[11] The Reverend William Studdert Kennedy did not neglect his parishioners, and Mozley also noted that he had a core of loyal, working-class worshippers. This must have affected Geoffrey. Michael Grundy, in his book on Geoffrey, commented that during the days at St Mary's:

*Here was born his profound affection for the poor... he was always to feel genuinely at home amongst them. He saw the strong bonds of community and comradeship that waited them and discovered that though they might be poor*

*materially, they were rich in spirit. His whole life was to
be committed to the further fulfilment and enrichment of
such lives.*[12]

It is important to note that his concern for the working class did
not start when he was a chaplain. From childhood onwards, it was
as though he was being prepared for it.

Geoffrey started his formal schooling at the age of nine, when
he joined a small private school run by a Mr Knightly. At some
point, probably with the aid of coaching from Knightly, he also
studied for Trinity College, Dublin, where it was possible to take
its exams without being a regular resident. It is of interest that by
2012 the college did list him as one of its well-known students.

At the age of fourteen, he transferred to Leeds Grammar
School under the headship of the Reverend John Henry Dudley
Matthews. The school was over three centuries old and was local,
independent, and for day pupils. The number of boys had declined
in the 1880s and Matthews was appointed in 1884. Educated
at Rugby and Oxford University, he was only forty but already
had experience as a headmaster. He improved the libraries, the
conditions of the buildings, the teaching of languages, and put an
emphasis on science. By 1896, the roll showed 161 pupils. Fees
were modest and thirty-five scholarships were available, and it is
possible that Geoffrey obtained one of these.

He soon settled as a bright student ready to participate in all
the school's activities. A school contemporary, Alfred Thompson,
commented that Geoffrey was "a very valuable member of the
school, a fellow with a really good brain, a hardworking and
intelligent Rugger forward with plenty of strength and grit, and
a good long distance runner. He was by no means a bad gymnast,
being very evenly balanced in bodily development."[13] In the 1901
school sports competition he won the quarter mile race.

Nor was he just interested in sport: he was also a leading
member of the school's Literary and Debating Society, and
during his last debate there, according to Mozley, he seconded

the opposition to the motion "That England has mainly herself to thank for her unpopularity abroad". Mozley then quotes from the school magazine, which said that "he made an excellent speech, which again took the debate out of the domain of hard fact to the region of abstract ideas". Commenting on his school career overall, Mozley added:

> *Leeds Grammar School meant a great deal to Geoffrey. He worked hard and he played hard and entered fully and gladly into the school's corporate life. It would not be true to say that he made many close friends, but it was always natural for him to like and admire people, just as I think it has always been impossible for anyone who has come to know him at all well not to like and admire him. To his school contemporaries he was always probably a bit of a wild Irishman but I think that those of us who knew him best realized something of the intellectual ability which lay behind his oddities. And from quite an early stage in my friendship with him I was struck with the fineness of his character.*[14]

In his last year, the headmaster offered a prize for the best poem. Geoffrey entered and Mozley, who read it, thought it of a high standard. He did not win, but the poem may have been the first serious poem by the man who was to become famous for his rhymes.

At the end of 1901, Geoffrey left school to concentrate on the subjects he had started at Trinity College, Dublin, the institution his father had attended. As an external student, he had completed some preliminary examinations. He now went full-time and obtained a first class degree in classics and divinity.

# 2

## INTO THE CHURCH, 1905–14

### Schoolteacher

In 1905, at the age of twenty-one, Geoffrey obtained a post as
a schoolteacher at Calday Grange Grammar School in West
Kirby. The school was founded in 1636 and still exists today as a
technology college. Little is known about this period, and Geoffrey
himself makes no written reference to it. William Purcell, writing
in 1962, states, "He was there two and a half years, happily content
teaching classics and general subjects."[1] He also took games and
enjoyed boxing, a skill with which he was later to surprise and
impress fellow soldiers.

Purcell also noted: "The years of teaching at Calday Grange
were happy enough, a period of vigorous, disordered reading,
an extension in adult life of the habit of childhood."[2] He draws
attention to Geoffrey's interest

> in what was known as the New Psychology, in subjects which
> were on the whole for the most advanced of Edwardians,
> still a fair way beyond the pale even of conversation. It
> was an interest however which persisted with Geoffrey,
> and emerged in later times, in his books The Warrior, The
> Woman and the Christ and I Pronounce Them.[3]

These New Psychology books included those by Havelock Ellis
and Sigmund Freud.

Mozley kept in touch and wrote, "I have reason to believe
that he liked the life and was popular with the boys."[4] They
spent holidays together and in August 1905, along with brother
Maurice, they cycled from Leeds to London via Rugby, Leicester,

and Buckingham. In 1906, Geoffrey and Mozley spent the Easter vacation exploring Port Sunlight in the Wirral. This was a village created by the successful soap manufacturers, William Lever and his brothers, who wanted to provide good quality housing for their workers and their families. Starting in 1889, they built Port Sunlight, a healthy and stimulating environment. There were 850 houses, accommodating 3,500 residents. In addition there were schools, a church, a hospital, leisure facilities, and an art gallery. Geoffrey may well have been impressed by the good relationships between employer and employees there, for it was something he urged in his later writings.

During the evenings the two men engaged in deep discussions, especially on theological subjects, and Mozley noted, "I find it hard to conceive a time when his eyes were not fixed on the priesthood as his life's work."[5]

As J. K. Mozley indicated, Geoffrey was considering the priesthood. The Church of England was going through a difficult period at this time. Church attendance was in decline, particularly in urban areas and among working-class people. In his masterly book, *The Church of England and the First World War*, Alan Wilkinson cites one of the few radical bishops, Charles Gore, who stated: "The bishops' incomes linked them with the wealthy. The clergy sought their friends among the gentry and professional people. So clerical opinions and prejudices reflected those of the upper and middle classes, not those of wage earners."[6] Sir Robert Ensor noted a drop in the very able candidates for the ministry and attributed it not just to growing doctrinal doubts but also to rival careers that were "fast developing – the new civil service, the new openings in education and research, the higher journalism and a variety of business callings". [7]

These changes did not alter Geoffrey's determination to be a priest. He was born and bred an Anglican and so knew its traditions and services. More importantly, he had a living faith. Following their conversations during the holidays, Mozley commented, "What impressed me in these talks was his sense of what the Christian gospel demanded of him personally."[8] Geoffrey concluded that God was calling him into the Anglican ministry and in October 1907 he entered Ripon Clergy College.

## Ripon Clergy College

The college was founded in 1896 by William Boyd Carpenter, Bishop of Ripon. A famous cleric, he was Canon of Windsor, Clerk to the Closet of Edward VII and on speaking terms with European royalty. His high connections did not stop him having a concern for working-class people, and he had founded the college partly in order to improve the quality of the clergy who ministered to them. A renowned preacher himself, he took a close interest in the students and advised them on the development of their speaking abilities. Purcell records his reaction to Geoffrey:

> *Here was something different; here was something, in this Irish voice, this intensity of real power. One thing, however was clear: the man was unique, could be fitted into no mould. As regards instruction in the art of preaching, Studdert Kennedy, in fact, was best left alone to develop in his own way.*[9]

One of the students with whom Geoffrey became friendly was A. T. Woodman-Dowding who, years later, became vice-principal of the college. In writing about Geoffrey's time there, he commented that he was particularly influenced by a course in the philosophy of religion delivered by a Dr Major. He added: "Some years ago, Kennedy confessed to the writer that the thought of which his life and services were expressions, and of which his books are illustrations, was in the first instance derived from Dr Major's lectures."[10] He concluded, "Both in his conversations and his preaching, Kennedy certainly impressed his contemporaries, who, in the manner of young men, repressed rather than welcomed emotion, with the indubitable fact that he was a man possessed by some force or influence that would not let him go."[11]

Geoffrey Studdert Kennedy had been outspoken, even boisterous, at home and school. He was not so at college. The college principal, Canon Battersby-Harford, described him as "a quiet and self-contained, able man" but, like Boyd Carpenter and the students, saw something special in him and added that "one felt that underneath there were gifts and fire which in crisis would blaze out".[12] These were prophetic words. Geoffrey completed the one-year course successfully and in 1908 was ordained deacon in Worcester Cathedral and then sent to work in Rugby, which was in the Worcester diocese.

## Rugby Parish Church

Rugby had been a market town best known for its famous public school where rugby football was invented. The arrival of the railways in the nineteenth century resulted in Rugby becoming a great railway centre. Industries multiplied and the population increased from 2,500 in 1833 to over 10,000 in 1880. Geoffrey was sent to St Andrew's, the parish church of Rugby. It had existed since the thirteenth century and its magnificent structure drew many visitors. The church was one of the most notable in the country. It had had just two rectors in the previous seventy-five years – John Moultre and John Murray – both of whom, according to Purcell, had been outstanding leaders. Although based at St Andrew's, Geoffrey was also expected to work in other churches in the area.

The church had a large team of curates. Some of these were what William Purcell calls "the officer class of the Anglican ministry",[13] those whose public school and Oxbridge backgrounds destined them for quick promotion. Geoffrey had a much more humble upbringing but this did not deter him and, to cite Purcell again, he "dropped upon the parish like a bomb making a small crater in the collective memory".[14] The rector was Dr Albert Victor Baillie, a godson of Queen Victoria, and well known in Rugby and beyond. He proved to be a wise and gracious leader who moulded his staff into an effective and friendly team.

Rugby was a prosperous town but also had many in poverty. Recent reforms by the Liberal government had introduced unemployment pay for short periods for a limited number of occupations and old age pensions for some – certainly not all – elderly people. However, many people with insufficient funds to feed and house themselves had to apply to the Poor Law, whose locally elected guardians might give stringent out-relief or receive the destitute into workhouses. The Rugby Workhouse had opened in 1819 and was usually full of paupers who had no means of supporting themselves. During 1905, it was full, with a daily average attendance of 148. Husbands were separated from wives and children from their parents. Conditions inside these institutions were made harsh in order to deter applicants. George Lansbury, an Anglican Christian, was elected a Guardian in Poplar. He wrote of its workhouse, "Everything possible was done to inflict mental and moral degradation."[15]

At this stage, Geoffrey had not developed an interest in politics nor his criticisms of the Poor Law. Like his father, he concentrated on helping poor people through the church. Unlike some of his colleagues, Geoffrey was at ease with people in the slums. He chose to spend much time in the poorest neighbourhoods. At times he helped the poorest with money from his pocket or clothes from his wardrobe. One of his fellow curates was Percy Herbert, who wrote about him:

> *I can see him again that small slim figure strolling into the unattractive public houses where his beloved lodging house tramps were to be found, and standing up in the bar in his cassock to sing Nazareth while half his audience "felt within a power unfelt before" – they loved him for his great laugh, the smile that transformed his face, the inimitable Irish brogue, but most of all because of his love for them. He was entirely at home in the dirtiest of kitchens, and would sit for hours smoking or watching by a sickbed.*[16]

After he had been in Rugby for one year, he received a visit from his brother Hugh, who himself had been a curate in the same church.

Hugh wrote about his visit:

> *His work at Rugby was typical of his work everywhere.*
> *He was literally aflame with divine love. "Go out into the*
> *highways and byways and compel them to come in." Those*
> *early days of his ministry at Rugby, where he at once began*
> *to make a name for himself first made me realise that he was*
> *destined to go far.*[17]

Geoffrey's living rooms were over a butcher's shop in the High Street. The premises included a room where he and his colleagues allowed children to play – often in their bare feet. Dr Baillie was anxious to extend the outreach of the church and chose Geoffrey to run a new mission in the middle of the poorest area. It was located in an abandoned Nonconformist chapel not far from the parish church, and soon became the hub of his work. On Sunday afternoons he started a gathering for children under the age of seven. Soon, 200–300 gathered to learn verses, sing songs, and chant prayers. Birthdays were always noted and celebrated. Finally, they listened to a story told by Geoffrey in his enthralling style. In the evening, he held a mission service for local adults and his friends from the lodging houses. They felt comfortable with him and were ready just to wander in to the mission to chat with him.

He also took services at Holy Trinity Church, which attracted a large congregation of elderly ladies who liked a comfortable service and sermon. On one occasion, he startled them by declaring that the Epistle of St Jude was the most repulsive document in the New Testament. In a subsequent sermon, he declared he would like to smash the stained glass windows with a sledgehammer and celebrate the Lord's Supper in the fields. Many of the windows in the church had been installed in the memory of relatives, and his fiery words upset some worshippers, who complained to Dr Baillie. In fact, Geoffrey did appreciate stained glass windows. His point, which somehow got lost, was that externals should not replace our love for God but should be an expression of it.

Once in the pulpit, Geoffrey kept the attention of the congregation. He always wanted to preach, but not to magnify himself. On the contrary, a number of his contemporaries noted his humility. He was just driven to take the Christian gospel and Christian teaching to others. He had the capacity to hold those who attended the mission. And not only them; masters from Rugby School were also drawn to hear him in church.

For all his preaching, in which he often drew upon the books he was reading, his friend J. K. Mozley says that at this stage he was still not a constructive thinker: "He was very sensitive to ideas, and though it would be untrue to say that he lacked a critical faculty, it was easier for him to absorb than to reject."[18] Yet there was one school of thought which he did reject. Several of his brothers had turned to Christian Science. J. K. Mozley adds:

> *Geoffrey was powerfully attracted by ideas which we associate with Christian Science. And if he did not become a Christian Scientist, which was the case with some of his brothers and sisters, that was in no small measure due to the wisdom with which his views were treated.*[19]

It may well have been that the wisdom came from Dr Baillie. He was well satisfied with Geoffrey and had no hesitation in recommending him to the priesthood. He was subsequently ordained on 29 May 1910 in the Collegiate Church of St Michael, Coventry, by the Bishop of Worcester.

## Back to Leeds

Geoffrey's mother died in March 1908. An inscription in her memory placed on the wall at St Mary's Church (which was demolished in 1979) read, "A good example to us all during 30 years as wife, mother and friend." His widowed and elderly father increasingly felt the strain of his work, and in 1912 Geoffrey felt that God was calling him to move back to Leeds to support him. His request was granted. He was made part of a team of curates attached to Leeds Parish Church but freed to be a curate to his father.

The Reverend Dr Samuel Bickersteth, whose son Kenneth had been a curate alongside Geoffrey in Rugby, served as vicar of the parish church of St Peter-at-Leeds from 1905 to 1916 and subsequently spoke warmly of Geoffrey's pastoral work and preaching. He wrote:

> *What strikes me most about this test of his character was the loyalty it revealed in him: loyalty to his aged father, still at the vicarage: loyalty to the bishop and to me... most of all, loyalty to his own conscientious convictions and ever-deepening sympathy with the under-dog.*[20]

An unnamed woman from the Leeds parish confirmed his concern for the poor by saying, "He prepared me for confirmation. He looked after the poor of the parish. I knew people he gave a pint of milk a day because they could not afford it."[21]

At this time, Christianity in Leeds was subjected to organized verbal attacks from atheists, often in the open air. Mostly the gatherings took place in an open space at Victoria Square, right in the centre of the city, close to the railway station. Crowds assembled around the statues of Queen Victoria, Wellington, and Peel to listen to the orators. The church responded by putting up its own speakers, including some eminent academics. Geoffrey was also to the fore in front of the crowds, and Bickersteth wrote:

> *I can recollect none who more instantly caught the attention of the crowd of up-turned faces, sometimes 100, sometimes 1000, lit up by the glare of the electric light, than Geoffrey Studdert Kennedy. Whenever I sent for him to speak, probably nothing gave him greater pleasure, as he and a crowd were born to react on each other. If "they thowt, he was only a pup because of his short tail", alluding to his short coat, they also knew he could bark, and if need be bite, never viciously but with vigour.*[22]

He revelled in the atmosphere, the remarks from the crowd, and the opportunity to interact with those who never entered a church.

It was not all services and preaching to crowds. Geoffrey was to fall in love with Emily Catlow. Other authors say little about her, but the censuses reveal some interesting material. She was born in 1888, six years after her brother John Harris Catlow. Her father Charles Alfred Catlow was a coal merchant who had been born in 1860. In 1880, he married Julia Lucas whose family were located in both Hereford and Leeds. The indications are that the marriage was not a happy one, for they did not always live together.

What of Emily? In 1891, she was with neither parent but was living with her uncle John Lucas (her mother's brother) and her maternal grandmother. By 1911, she was caring for the grandmother in Leeds and her occupation was given as a governess. Nothing is known about her education but she did play the piano and always had an interest in Shakespeare. At some point, she moved to be with an aunt in Leeds. At this time, her mother Julia was also in Leeds with Emily's sister Elizabeth.

Her brother John was in Leeds training to be a solicitor. John met Geoffrey Studdert Kennedy when they played in opposing teams in a football match. They became friends and John introduced him to the dark, attractive Emily. A relationship developed and it so happened that she was on holiday in Scarborough at the same time as Geoffrey was leading a boys' camp there. She was brave enough to accompany him in the otherwise all-male meetings and they both sang at the camp concert. They must have spent some time alone, for Emily accepted his proposal of marriage. They were married on 25 April 1914 at St Mary's Quarry Hill with her brother John as a signatory on the wedding certificate. The service was conducted by the Reverend J. K. Mozley, who later said that Emily "was the lady who has been to Studdert Kennedy so true a helpmate".[23]

Not long after the wedding, Geoffrey's father William died at the age of eighty-eight. Typically, he had not retired and was still in harness until his end. An entry in the England and Wales National Probate Calendar shows that he left the not inconsiderable sum of £475. It all went to Geoffrey. A delegation from the parish requested of the church authorities that Geoffrey should succeed his father. The request was refused, perhaps because the authorities felt that a change from the Studdert Kennedys was required. Geoffrey was not aggrieved. His preaching was making him noted and he received three offers from other churches. One was from St Paul's Church in Worcester, and a report reveals that he said to his wife, "St Paul's has the smallest income and the poorest people – go and look at the house and, if you think you can manage it, I will accept."[24] The house – it still stands – was located among factories and poor housing. Emily gladly approved and her husband accepted the post with the salary of £300 a year and a parish of over 4,000 people. He started on 9 June 1914. A few weeks later, Britain declared war against Germany.

# 3

# WORCESTER AND WAR, 1914–16

Studdert Kennedy was instituted as vicar of St Paul's on 9 June 1914. Worcester was a historical city, once a Roman settlement, scene of two major battles in the Civil War in the seventeenth century, and dominated by a magnificent cathedral.

His new church also had a history. Its full name was St Paul's in the Blockhouse, an area outside the city wall developed in the early nineteenth century. The first St Paul's was constructed between 1835 and 1837, but, as the parish grew in industry, housing, and population, soon a larger church was required. In 1877, Canon Henry Douglas became vicar. The son of an earl, he and his wife, Lady Mary Douglas, made plans for a larger church to which they devoted much of their own money. Designed by a distinguished church architect, George Street – and, after his death, completed by his son Arthur – the new St Paul's was opened in 1886. The second largest church in Worcester, it could accommodate over a thousand people.

Built in the medieval gothic style of the fourteenth century, it had three large perpendicular windows in the west wall. In a short history of the architecture of the church, Christopher Hart writes, "The blending of stone and brick in the exterior is both excellent and simple. Every line is firmly structured."[1] Father Geoffrey, as he became known in the parish, soon grew to love the beauty of the building.

The Reverend P. T. R. Kirk wrote of him, "He was a High Churchman who loved ritual as an aid to worship."[2] But only as an aid, a means of drawing nearer to a personal God. He started nearly every day with Holy Communion at 7 a.m. no matter how late he had been up or how tired he felt. The bread and wine were a constant reminder of the suffering that Christ endured for humankind.

On Sunday evenings, he led evensong. Paul Tongue, a Canon Emeritus at Worcester Cathedral, a local expert on Geoffrey Studdert

Kennedy, comments, "At St Paul's, evensong ceased to be a service and became an experience – a service alive with passion and earnestness. And that wonderful preaching."[3] When Father Geoffrey preached, the lights were dimmed so worshippers would not be distracted by those around them while he broke a golden rule of preaching, to maintain eye contact with the congregation, and instead spoke with his eyes fixed on one of the high windows. People came again and again to the church.

After the services, scores of worshippers would queue to speak with him about what he had been saying, about finding God, about prayer, about their own sins. He turned none away. And not just in church. In the parish magazine which accompanied his first services, he wrote, "My study is a place where anyone can come in and talk and be sure of a hearty welcome. I do want to be a friend of everyone."[4] People took him at his word and Michael Grundy wrote, "A constant tide of folk came to the doors of the large vicarage – not just regular members of the congregation, but the lonely, the anxious, alcoholics, the suicidal, drug takers, the conscience-laden and the penniless."[5] Sometimes, late in the evenings, his wife Emily had to rescue him in order to ensure that he did get some sleep.

Father Geoffrey also gave care and attention to child baptisms and funerals. At the former, he sometimes read his own poems, which were probably the forerunners of his rhymes which were to be best-sellers. The funerals were occasions to be remembered by mourners as he entered into their grief with tears in his own eyes. Some were led to continue attending the church.

Although content to remain in the parish, at times he left in order to take retreats held at the chapel in Earl Beauchamp's house near Malvern or at the Deanery in Worcester. These often drew in Christians of a higher social class than his flock at St Paul's. He held their attention and deepened their spirituality, and his reputation as a speaker grew.

## Father Geoffrey and the Poor

Hart explains that the church "was built in a working class area, and the parish that it served was the smallest, poorest and roughest in the city".[6] It stood in the midst of back-to-back terraced housing. Every group of twelve houses shared one toilet and washroom. Many residents found employment in nearby factories, including the Royal Worcester Porcelain Company, Williamson's Tin Plate Works, Hardy and Padmore's Foundry, Hill Evans' Vinegar Factory, and Fownes' Glove Factory. Wages were generally low.

As in Rugby and Leeds, Father Geoffrey gave priority to the poor. Part of most days he knocked on the doors of the terraced houses. A local woman remembered:

> *The first thing that Mr Kennedy did was to visit all the poor people. He was all for the poor. Also he had exceptional skills as a spiritual advisor. A steady flow of men and women found a man who thought it a privilege to take upon himself their burdens and their sins.*[7]

In particular, he visited the sick whether they attended the church or not.

His generosity brimmed over. He regularly took groceries to the needy. He did not charge to marry those on low incomes. The best-known story tells that, finding an aged invalid lying on an uncomfortable couch, he brought a pillow from the vicarage, then sheets, then parts of a bed. Finally, with the aid of Emily, he brought the mattress. It was their own bed, so the Kennedys had to sleep on cushions.

The Reverend William Moore Ede, the Dean of Worcester, revealed that "Some people have commented severely on Kennedy's want of financial prudence". He then draws on some words of the Reverend John Hunt, who was Studdert Kennedy's colleague at St Paul's. He explained:

> *It was not the fact that he did not know the meaning or value of money; he did and with a deep understanding of its use and limits which will come as a surprise to many people. He did not develop the "acquisitive instinct", and this made him shed*

*not only his own money but his possessions everywhere. He was, however, never reckless with other people's money. He was studiously careful to see that parochial monies, donations and any gifts entrusted to him were used to the best possible advantage. He supervised the expenditure and had faithful accounts rendered to him, and he gave careful and prayerful thought for the wise use thereof. He was often perplexed as to where funds were coming from to help the (literally) hundreds of people he had on his heart for every conceivable need, lifting up girls and women from the results of moral falls, helping to educate promising children of poor parents, in emigrating families overseas, restarting from ruin those who had failed.*[8]

Canon Paul Tongue again puts it well. He acknowledged that a previous vicar, Canon Henry Douglas and his wife Lady Douglas, gave much of their fortune to the church. He continued, "But in terms of the Lord's parable of the widow's mite, they gave of their superfluity. Father Geoffrey gave his all. If the Douglases went three miles, Father Geoffrey went four."[9]

Moore Ede also observed, "Children are quick to perceive and understand those who really love them, and the children of St Paul's loved the vicar who loved them and flocked round him as he went about the parish."[10] Sometimes he gave them a penny to get into the picture house. At other times, it was sixpence for nuts and pomegranates from the local fruit shop. Michael Grundy interviewed an elderly man who, as a child, knew the vicar and said, "After choir practices he would visit us in the hut and taught us boxing. He was very good and had a wicked left."[11]

Father Geoffrey built up a large Sunday school. He also took a close interest in the local day school where the pupils were always glad to greet him. The teachers were probably welcoming as well for, in a school designed for 236 children, 328 were in attendance.

He was keen to have a social club to serve the area and persuaded the Church Army to start one. It was run by a captain and his wife who moved into the vicarage with the Kennedys. Father Geoffrey encouraged them to open boys' and girls' clubs and was often found in the clubs himself. Such services as these were open to all parishioners whether members of the church or not. This did not dim his desire to see people commit themselves to Christianity and to this end he often preached the gospel in the open air.

In his initial years as vicar at St Paul's, Father Geoffrey confirmed his power as a preacher, developed his abilities to organize a parish church, revealed his gift for making personal relationships, and continued his concern for the poor. But already, his ministry at St Paul's was being overshadowed by the war.

## Origins of the First World War

The origins of the First World War in which Britain and her allies became locked in combat with Germany and her allies are well explained by Professor Gary Sheffield.[12] Whatever the reasons for the war, A. J. P. Taylor shows that it was welcomed in Britain almost with "hysteria", with all the major political parties giving it their backing.[13] Father Geoffrey was among the many supporters of the war.

In Britain, the majority of church denominations approved the declaration of war. The Archbishop of Canterbury, Randall Davidson, backed war, although more cautiously than some other church leaders. The Bishop of London, Arthur Winnington-Ingram, for instance, often appeared in military uniform and his rallying calls were said to have recruited 10,000 to the army. Cardinal Bourne of the Catholic Church, Frederick B. Meyer on behalf of the free churches, and the Chief Rabbi and other prominent church spokesmen added their support. A report in the Worcester Cathedral Archives shows that local Church of England and Nonconformist churches welcomed the taking up of arms.[14]

## Father Geoffrey Enters the War

Father Geoffrey voiced his backing for the war. He had no sympathy for conscientious objectors. In the first parish magazine after war started, he wrote:

*I cannot say too strongly that I believe every able-bodied man ought to volunteer for service anywhere. There ought to be no shirking of that duty. Those who cannot volunteer for military service can pray. Let us work and pray. It remains for us to keep a brave face, to shed our tears in secret and wear our smiles in public, to be sober and chivalrous in victory and patient and steady in defeat.*[15]

Despite his devotion to St Paul's, he applied to enlist as a chaplain. That could not happen at once. Father Geoffrey had to be approved by the military authorities, and someone, approved by the bishop, had to be found to replace him. While he waited, the army came to him. Just outside Worcester stood the extensive Norton Barracks Established in 1877, it was the home of the Worcester Regiment, and was to train over 10,000 soldiers during the course of the war. On Sundays, the recruits marched to the cathedral for church parade. The Dean of Worcester, the Reverend William Moore Ede, had a high opinion of Father Geoffrey's preaching skills and asked him to deliver some of the sermons. Could he do it? Speaking in the open air to listeners who chose to be there was one thing. Holding the attention of masses of working-class men who were ordered to attend was another. Ede recorded, "Each time he went into the pulpit and spoke to those two thousand unwilling listeners, he held them spellbound – not a cough, no shuffling of feet. What he said became the main topic of conversation during the ensuing week."[16]

On 21 December 1915, Father Geoffrey was appointed a chaplain. Within four days, he was conducting a Christmas Day service in a village square in France. The rain poured down on 400 soldiers but it did not dampen their singing as they rendered the carols. Writing to a Worcester newspaper, he explained:

*Then the glorious part came – I went to a shed in the farmyard and the communicants came to me. There were not many; but they meant it. No lights, no ritual, nothing to help but the rain and the far-off roll of guns, and Christ was born in a cattle shed on Christmas day.*[17]

By 1 January 1916, Father Geoffrey had been posted to the town of Rouen where he spent most of his time in a large shed on a railway siding. It had been turned into a canteen in which soldiers on their way to the front waited – perhaps for twenty-four hours – for their train.

What was he to do? Chaplains received little if any training. Surrounded by soldiers, he mounted a box and sang "Mother Macree" for the sons, "My Little Grey Home in the West" for husbands, and "The Sunshine of Your Smile" for lovers. Father Geoffrey possessed not only a fine voice but also a sincerity that gripped his listeners. He prayed for those at home and then helped some to write letters to their loved ones. He found a line of men wanting to talk with him, perhaps about problems, perhaps just to show him photographs of their wives and children. Finally they were ordered into a crowded train, often with no washing facilities. Father Geoffrey then walked up and down giving away New Testaments from one bag and Woodbines from another. The train puffed away and he watched until its lights disappeared. He wondered how many of their lives would also disappear. Thereafter he was known as Woodbine Willie.

On one occasion, he met a number of troops from Worcester. In a letter sent to his parishioners at St Paul's, he wrote:

> *I struck a good many Worcester fellows the other day who knew me as soon as they heard My Little Grey Home in the West and came through the crowd round the piano to shake hands. One lad named Baddely was at the first informal recruiting meeting which Frank Stanway and I held just after the war broke out, and enlisted just afterwards. I also came across some wireless men from just behind the vicarage. I wrote home for most of these.*[18]

Half a century later in a report in a local Worcester paper, the then elderly Arthur Savage told how Father Geoffrey wrote on his behalf to his wife and that she still treasured the letter.

In another letter to his church, Father Geoffrey explained that he also served some troops quartered in the town and said, "… it is sad because here is the old enemy one fights – sin – and sin is sadder than sorrow."[19] He was talking about alcohol and sex. He continued:

> *Had I a boy I would pray that he might never be long at base. He is surrounded by temptations, and has to fight every inch of his way, if he is to live a clean life… The temptations to vice are appalling, and it is a great chance to help… In your prayers remember the men at the base… Lord, how angry it makes me this attack on men in the rear. Better the guns of the Germans than the temptations of the Devil. I am glad to be here and yet I hate it. Some men lead heroic lives but many fall and lose what they can never gain again, save by the grace of God and the absolution of the Church.*[20]

On a brighter note, the local mayor gave permission for lectures to be given at the large Grande Salle in the Hotel de Ville. Father Geoffrey delivered a series of Lenten talks. The meetings started with music from an orchestra for twenty minutes and then it was all him. He mixed religion with patriotism, which inspired the men. He held the attention of the soldiers and was always applauded and cheered. His ability to preach and encourage, to make his listeners laugh, weep, and cheer must have been noticed by senior officers and chaplains.

## The Front Line

Father Geoffrey himself was soon to be transported to the front line for one of the most important and longest battles of the war. The Somme, which was the name of a French department as well as a river, covered a key area through which the German army could make a breakthrough. The Allies' plan was that heavy preliminary bombardment would rupture the German lines, so that an advance could be made through the resulting gap, which would then spread out. The drawback, according to the historian A. J. P. Taylor, was that "The senior officers were elderly, unimaginative professionals, who refused to contemplate the problems of trench warfare."[21]

They appeared to overlook that the enemy held higher and better protected land, had constructed hundreds of fortified machine gun posts, and had dug-outs so deep that they would be safe from anything except the heaviest shells.

The bombardment began on 1 July 1916. It could be heard in southern England and inflicted terrible damage on German trenches. The British infantry, with most facing battle for the first time, had waited in flooded trenches. They climbed out, weighed down by ammunition and tools amounting to 66 lb, and attacked. They made an initial advance but then found that much of the barbed wire in no-man's-land had not been destroyed and that the enemy machine gun nests were still active. Further, the enemy had concealed troops in holes and tunnels so that, once British soldiers had passed over, they emerged and shot them in the back. By the end of the day, 21,000 were killed and 35,000 injured – the greatest loss on a single day ever suffered by a British army. There was no breakthrough and both sides settled for a war of attrition in which smallish gains and losses were made.

What was the battle like for the first-time participant, Father Geoffrey? Soon after the fighting, he described his baptism of fire. "We were preparing for the Great Offensive. I had just come up to the front as Chaplain to the —— Brigade. I had never seen a trench and never heard a gun go off."[22] The men told him that they were to dig a kick-off trench out in front of their front line – and all in pouring rain. Father Geoffrey decided he had to go with them. He followed them to a battered village from which communication trenches ran to the front line. Then into these trenches wading waist deep in water. The men entered the blackness of no-man's-land to dig the next trench, the silence broken by the sound of machine guns and the occasional shell. After two hours, the captain in charge asked Father Geoffrey to move to the men to see if he could cheer them up. He wrote:

*Fear came. There was a pain underneath my belt. Of course, I had to go. It was the parish. We crept out. We could not get out into the two-foot ditch that they had made, it was crowded with men. We went along the edge. I whispered some inane remark as I passed by, and was rewarded with a grin which even darkness could not hide, and often when I had passed with the muttered comment, "Gaw blyme me if it ain't the padre!" Vaguely I felt that this journey was worthwhile.*[23]

Some German flares went over, a warning of what was to come.

*You'd better get into the trench, Padre, whispered the Captain. I was in it before he said it. I never moved so quickly in my life. There was silence for what seemed an age and must have been a minute. The men had ceased to dig. Then a hail of machine gun bullets burst over us with a noise like bitter hatred and foul words. A cry or a grunt here and there told me that some men were hit. Then it stopped, and I could hear nothing but a voice close by muttering "God! God! God!" through set teeth with a swift hissing intake of breath between each word. Then like a sudden thunderstorm the shelling burst upon us… I can remember kneeling up to the waist in water watching the reflection of the bursting high explosive on the surface of it, saying the Lord's Prayer and wondering about Death, the beauty of the silver reflections, fear, and bloody mothers' meetings. Presently I mastered the terror in my inside and became more conscious of those around me. The man immediately in front of me had lost his nerve and was crying and pleading with God for mercy. The man behind me was better, he was swearing steadily at the Germans, and kicking me and saying between his oaths – "Go on! Go on!" "I can't go on," I shouted back; "the chap in front of me has got the hump or the blue jibbers or something." A tremendous kick was the reply, and then in tones of puzzled fury – "Who the hell's that?" The situation was getting comic. "This is the Church," I roared back. Then came the great question. "And what the —— —— is the Church doing here?"*[24]

The final battles of the Somme took place in September amidst sleet and snow. Both sides were exhausted. In one place, British troops had advanced seven miles but, generally, little territorial change had occurred. The Germans were worried that they now had to withdraw troops to deal with the Russian threat in the east. Nationally, it was difficult to say who were the winners. But there were over a million losers. In all, well over a million men were killed (600,000 French and British and 500,000 German).

However, much of his time was not spent in battles. The troops frequently marched long distances to new locations and he marched with them. Even more time was spent in waiting. This included digging trenches and tunnels, cleaning kit, taking turns at guard duty, and parades at which their weapons and clothes were inspected. Father Geoffrey was usually alongside them. He shared their meals, told jokes, led some singing. When he was asked questions about religion, he tried to answer them in language which could be understood. He did not call the men to prayer but, if any requested it, he was pleased to do so, usually asking God to look after their families back home.

Above all, he ensured that he was always present when the men prepared to go over the top. Inevitably, he distributed Woodbines. When the whistle blew for the advance, he was in the midst. Once over the top, the men usually faced bullets and shells, with many mown down. He then sought out the wounded and the dying. The former he often dragged out of the mud, got onto a stretcher, and pulled to the first aid post, ducking shells as they went. Sometimes he dragged the stretchers through flooded trenches. At times, he lay on his belly as he attempted to comfort the dying. After the fighting ceased, he returned to the makeshift hospital to remain with the badly wounded or to hold a man down as the doctor operated on him without anaesthetic. Often he went twenty-four hours without sleep and with little food. At times, he spluttered and coughed with his asthma. After the fighting, he gathered a few volunteers, and buried as many of the dead as could be found. He was still not finished; as soon as possible he wrote a personal letter to the relatives of the dead. Then, probably in September or October 1916, he was recalled from front line duty and found himself chosen for a different duty.

## Break Back Home

In October 1916, he had a short break back in Worcester. It may have been to consult with church leaders about his new duty. It may have been to recover from another attack of asthma. Certainly a part of one of his letters to Emily, sent earlier in 1916, is about his asthma and reads as follows. "My own darling Em, I have had rather a sharp attack of asthma which is now over. How I wish I could see the last of it. I have succeeded in throwing this off more quickly and I must be glad of that."[25]

In another letter, he had expressed his love for her, along with sadness at being apart, in poetry. It was entitled "Two Worlds".

> *In the valleys down below,*
> *Where the fairest flowers blow,*
> *And the brooks run babbling to the sea,*
> *Underneath the shady trees,*
> *We two sauntered at our ease.*
> *Just a pleasant little world for you and me.*
>
> *Then the summons of the Lord,*
> *Like a sudden silver sword,*
> *Came and cut our little pleasant world in two,*
> *One fierce world of strife and hate,*
> *One sad world where women wait,*
> *And we wander far apart, dear, I and you.*
>
> *And it may be, with this breath,*
> *There will come one call of death,*
> *And will put another world 'twixt you and me,*
> *You will stand with God above,*
> *I will stand 'twixt pride and love,*
> *Looking out through mists of sorrow o'er the sea.*

The poem was published later in his collection of rhymes called *Rough Rhymes of a Padre*. The break with Emily appears to have been short but sweet, for there is no record of him addressing the church.

# 4

# THE WANDERING PREACHER, 1916–17

Father Geoffrey's new task concerned the Church of England's response to the war. It had announced the National Mission for Repentance and Hope. The Archbishop of York, Cosmo Lang, explained to Convocation:

> *We have called it a National Mission for Repentance and Hope; Repentance because we are called to bid men and women everywhere to repent of the sins which have stained our civilisation and brought upon it the manifest judgement of God; and Hope because during the closing period of this terrific ordeal in the midst of increasing strain and sacrifice and sorrow, our people will need the strength of Hope, and in those difficult days that are coming, when the old order will have gone and the duty will be laid upon the nation of seeking a new order in a new world, we must present before the minds of the nation the one hope, Christ, His Mind, His Spirit, for the rebuilding of a new world.*[1]

Some of the sins identified were greed and selfishness, conflict between classes, drunkenness, and sexual immorality. The Mission wanted to include the soldiers who were fighting against Germany. It recognized that troops were making huge sacrifices and having their faith tested, even undermined. The decision was taken that the Mission should not only reach every parish in the home country but also the troops abroad.

But who could take the message of the Mission to the soldiers? By this time, Father Geoffrey had a reputation as a preacher who held the men's attention in services held in the open air – and sometimes in the rain – the day before battles. Officers and chaplains had reported this to the higher ranks of the clergy in Britain. An agreement between them and the army authorities led to Bishop Llewellyn Gwynne, deputy chaplain general, telling Father Geoffrey that he was the man. His immediate reaction was to protest that he wanted to stay at the front. In a letter written to his parishioners at St Paul's, he revealed that the bishop's response was, "It doesn't matter what you want. As you have been given by the Lord Almighty the gift of the gab you have to do as you are told."[2]

Despite his initial reluctance, Father Geoffrey agreed with the aims of the Mission and welcomed the opportunity to be a wandering preacher taking its message to many camps and bases. But he did not underestimate his task. He realized that working-class troops did not always see Christ in the same way as middle-class churchgoers. He knew that many from all classes struggled with the huge question of how a God of love could allow the terrible sufferings they saw around them, brought on by the war. The army senior officers made it clear to Father Geoffrey that, in addition to the objectives of the Mission, they wanted him to raise morale, reinforce patriotism, and increase the fighting spirit which some considered had declined in the face of huge losses of life. The initial plan was for him to preach at as many camps as possible. To this was added the role of acting as chaplain at four infantry training camps. These duties occupied him for much of the rest of the war.

From November 1916, Father Geoffrey worked at a tremendous rate. In a ten-day period, he preached three times a day to crowds of between 500 and 1,500. He then suffered a severe attack of his asthma, and had a temperature of 39.4 °C. After several weeks in hospital, he was sent to the south of France to rest. On recovery, he travelled back to the north of France; the temperature was −12 °C and the train took fourteen hours to cover forty-two miles. Once at the camp, he spent the evenings preaching to the troops and the days accompanying them in the front lines. By the end of April 1917, he had visited all the British bases.

Some of the army top ranks looked down upon Father Geoffrey socially, disapproved of the friendships he made with men who were not officers, and criticized some of the bawdy language in his sermons. One general, a devout Christian, reported him to a senior officer as a heretic. In fact, Geoffrey had been describing common but wrong images of God which he then corrected. Other officers admired him and developed a relationship with him. Above all, the ordinary soldiers heard him gladly.

The talks he gave were a huge success. At one camp, a passer-by was puzzled by the sight of soldiers outside a large hut, climbing up to windows and even onto the roof. It turned out that they were trying to hear Geoffrey speak. Professor Kerry Walters explains his popularity:

> When Studdert Kennedy preached he used the vernacular without lapsing into condescension. He cracked jokes, laughed at them, sat on the ledge of the platform with his legs dangling and used salty language... After his first few months of war experiences, he never tried to romanticize or glamorize the brutal, mucky, day-to-day task of soldiering. He was honest without being cynical, sympathetic without being sentimental.[3]

He knew that he had to grab the audience's attention with his first words. One favourite was, "I know what you're thinking: here comes the bloody parson." Another was, "You may have heard the story of the Irishman..." followed by the description of an Irishman watching a pub fight for some time then asking politely, "Excuse me, boss, but is this a proivate shindy or can any bloke join in?" A different slant was "Whenever I am inclined to lose faith in the British people and to believe that their day is done, there is one British institution that always restores my weakened faith and makes me proud again." That institution was not the House of Commons or the Church of England. "It is *Punch*." He would follow this introduction with a string of jokes from that magazine. He added that "so long as *Punch* remains what it is, king of all the comic papers in the world, so long, I believe, will Britain lead the nations in the march of the mind".[4]

## Rough Talks by a Padre

Does what he actually said still exist? None of his notes for talks survive but fortunately he used them in his first prose book *Rough Talks by a Padre*, published in 1918. It draws upon the Lent lectures he gave at Rouen in 1916 and the many succeeding talks at various camps. Father Geoffrey's previous biographers, William Purcell and Michael Grundy, do not give a detailed analysis of this book. It is not easy. The chapters may well have been written in a hurry and incorporate scores if not hundreds of talks. But six main themes are clear.

## British Innocence

Father Geoffrey argued that Britain was not to blame for the war and was fighting to preserve freedom and peace: the freedom of Belgium and the peace of Europe. The responsibility for the war rested wholly with Germany. He asserted that Britain was not a military nation, and gave as evidence the fact that the army had not been increased in the years leading up to the conflict. This was true, but Britain did engage in a naval arms race. It had long been British policy to have a navy twice the size of any other nation. This was partly because Britain had a vast empire to protect. In the early years of the twentieth century, Germany increased the strength of its navy as it too had designs on a larger empire. Britain responded and by 1914 it possessed twenty-seven dreadnoughts (very large battleships) against Germany's sixteen. Once the war started, the navy played a crucial part in the European war by transporting troops to France, blockading German ports, and engaging in naval battles which resulted in a huge loss of life.

He also argued that Britain's motive for waging war was not commercial expansion. The Labour leader, Keir Hardie, was one of the pre-war politicians who claimed that private companies were pushing the government to make war in order to increase their sales of arms, and he consistently argued that some manufacturers encouraged war, because it led to greater trade in arms, vehicles, and military uniforms. He had opposed the Boer War on the same grounds.[5] Later historians have also identified a commercial motive and Norman Lowe writes of a fear that "a German victory would endanger British trading interests and ruin the balance of power in Europe".[6]

Father Geoffrey overstated his case that Britain entered the war just to preserve freedom and peace. But it did want to protect Belgium and did see war as the means of eventually bringing peace to Europe. Father Geoffrey may have underestimated the economic reasons why Britain entered the war but he was convinced that it was for good motives and, addressing the troops, he told them they were fighting for freedom, honour, and the peace of the world.

### German Barbarism

His second point was that Germany was a barbaric nation which not only wanted but enjoyed war. It was driven by "unadulterated Barbarism" which sprang from its departure from Christianity, "the calm untroubled rejection by a whole people of the Christian basis of civilisation".[7] He concluded, "We are fighting to beat the Germans, and to beat them utterly: to beat them to their knees. We are fighting to force them into a position when they will humbly beg for mercy."[8]

Father Geoffrey's extreme view was not shared by all British Christians. Indeed, the Archbishop of Canterbury, Randall Davidson, while agreeing that the war against Germany was justified, was careful not to condemn all Germans. As Wilkinson commented, "He thought of Germany as a Christian nation and did not fall into the popular identification of Germany as anti-Christ or as a complete mass of barbarians."[9] Davidson spoke calmly in Canterbury Cathedral and the House of Lords. It was different for Father Geoffrey addressing hundreds of soldiers whose determination to fight he wished to maintain.

### Sportsmanship

Perhaps oddly in the midst of war, Father Geoffrey's third point concerned the issue of sportsmanship. He stated:

> *The sporting spirit, at its best, is the highest form of the*
> *Christian spirit attainable by men at our present stage of*

*development, and in that spirit is the only hope of civilisation.*
*The sportsman puts right before might. He hits and hits hard,*
*but never hits below the belt… The sportsman regards the*
*man who will foul to win as the most contemptible person*
*on earth and he is in that absolutely Christian.*[10]

He continues:

*The great German crime is the denial of this sporting spirit*
*and its universal application… There is only one law in these*
*matters, the law that the strong must trample on the weak. This*
*is precisely what the Allies deny. There is a referee, we say. There*
*is the eternal referee, the God of Freedom, Truth and Right.*[11]

As Walters puts it, "One of the book's most painful… claims was that the Tommy was morally superior to the Hun because of the sporting tradition… Germany's crime is its denial of this tradition and its universal application."[12] But Father Geoffrey provided no evidence to back his assertions. British troops were known to pick up wounded Germans and carry them to first aid. Others shot German prisoners. Interestingly, Richard Tawney dismissed the comparison of war with sport and sportsmanship. He wrote, "But in the letters of the rank and file who have spent a winter in the trenches, you will not find war described as 'sport'. It is a load that they carry with aching bones, hating it…"[13]

As we have seen from his schooldays, Father Geoffrey was an enthusiastic sports player. He participated in athletics, football and boxing. No doubt – despite what Tawney said – sport was a topic he could discuss with soldiers in the trenches. Those in his audience would prick up their ears when he mentioned sport, so he used it as a means of showing their moral superiority over the Germans. To Father Geoffrey, sport meant abiding by the rules, observing fair play, values that could then be applied to life in general. Germans, he argued, played less sport and therefore were morally inferior.

## Drink and Sex

The senior clerics in Britain who had initiated the Mission for Repentance and Hope and the top army officers in France were agreed that heavy drinking and sex outside of marriage were evils. The clerics regarded them as undermining Christian lives. The officers saw them as a scourge which wrecked fighting men. So Father Geoffrey was pleasing both sets of his superiors when he spoke and wrote, in his fourth point, against the evils with his usual gusto. In Worcester he had witnessed the harm that drunken fathers could wreak on families. In France, he met drunken soldiers who could hardly stand up. He declared, "Drink inflames the body and loosens the control of the mind… But I'm not out to make the world teetotal. I'm not against a man having a glass of beer for his dinner; It's having a bucket of beer for his supper that I complain about."[14] He also understood that soldiers, after short spells of battle, often endured weeks of boredom which drove them to the drinking houses in nearby villages. His reasonableness, his humour, and his firmness appealed to them.

The trouble with drink was that it made men more prone to illicit sex. Often prostitutes were available. Father Geoffrey attempted not to be too puritanical, saying, "Oh men, I am no cold, white-livered, passion-hating saint. I have loved, and I love now with all my body and all my soul."[15] However, he insisted that sex belonged within marriage: "The act of intercourse was meant to be the crown of manhood and the crown of womanhood complete."[16] But many of the young soldiers were not married and some wanted to experience sex before they were killed.

He gave most attention to the matter of sex with prostitutes, which was easily available. The likelihood of getting venereal disease was high and inflicted personal suffering and pain. It led to the loss of good fighting men. "The prevalence of venereal disease, both gonorrhoea and syphilis, among the troops is a continual source of anxiety and distress to those who lead the army. It constitutes a continual daily, weekly, drain of men from the fighting strength."[17] Not least, he wanted compassion for prostitutes who were themselves vulnerable to disease. Many of them were not regular prostitutes, but had turned to prostitution because they badly needed the money. Once the soldiers left, they lost this source of income, and could find themselves also looking after children. Father Geoffrey was less strong on solutions to the problems. He said, "I am not going to lead a new movement with a new name: Kennedy's Anti-drink Crusade or Padre's Prisoners of Purity."[18] But he did have one unusual suggestion. Troops should get together to help and encourage each other concerning drink and sex. Long before group work and self-help groups became popular, he was advocating them. And he was advocating them at a time when sexual matters, especially sexual disease, were not bluntly and openly discussed by clergymen.

## The Role of the Church in a Time of War

Father Geoffrey, in his fifth point, tried to answer the question put to him in the trench, "What the ——— ——— is the Church doing here?" His short answer was, "It is trying to keep the hope of Heaven alive in the midst of a bloody Hell. It is trying to fill the army and to keep it filled with the Spirit of the Cross, the spirit of strong love of Right which will triumph at all costs in the battle against wrong."[19] Further, the church has to counter "the temptation for men to become brutalised and to live as do the brutes. The Spirit of the Bayonet without the Spirit of the Cross."[20] He had observed soldiers who, under the pressure of war, had retreated into a despair or indifference which led them to adopt a cruelty they would not have been guilty of before. He believed this could be avoided if they had a fuller understanding and experience of Christianity. Perhaps most difficult, the church had to enable troops to understand the mystery of suffering, of why a God of love allowed agony, cruelty, and death on a scale never known before. This was a problem to which he was to return again and again. Here he claims that historically it is "only by the suffering of the innocent that any lasting good for man was ever gained at all… the noble army of martyrs, the men who have suffered torture undeserved for the sake of Truth and Right".[21] He continued that the greatest and most undeserved suffering was that of Jesus Christ on the cross. He writes, "The Cross was a crime and the centre of a thousand crimes, and yet it is the source from which a cleansing stream of Justice, Love and Pity has flowed forth to heal the world."[22] In the same way, troops had to suffer now in order to win a better future for their families, their country, their world. If Jesus brought about spiritual salvation by his suffering, they could bring about social salvation by theirs.

### How the Future Will Be Won

His sixth theme asks about that better future. He acknowledged that the task looked immense, given that many in Britain were already poor and that the war had cost millions. The church had an important part to play. Unusually, he went outside the Church of England to say that he was addressing all denominations. For all churches were concerned with values and, if poverty was to be tackled, then the sin of avarice had to be overcome. He pronounced:

> *We must learn to hate with a bitter lasting hatred the idolatry of wealth… We took it for granted that man was made to make money, that true happiness could be bought… It has spoiled the spirit of our people, weakened our Government, and corrupted our institutions.*[23]

His point was that a nation without avarice would use its resources for the benefit of all.

Until this point, Father Geoffrey has said little about party politics or the means of government, but now he gives it some consideration. He believed that the war had brought about a unity in government which had focused solely on winning the war. In a small section, he argues that the new Britain must also have a unity which goes beyond political parties. Britain must "secure leaders who have no party to serve, and no axe to grind, no class to consider – men wholly devoted to the solution of these problems for the salvation of Great Britain and the welfare of the world – men who are clean at heart".[24] He does not explain how they are to be appointed or elected.

The content and tone of Father Geoffrey's talks and first book have come in for some criticism. At times, he is almost a mouthpiece for the views of the church and army establishments. His biographer, William Purcell, who admired him, nevertheless points out that "he seems at times to be used as a morale-booster to an extent which would certainly have been regarded as improper in a chaplain of the second world war".[25] Another admirer, Kerry Walters, writes that "in later years the book's jingoistic support of the war embarrassed Studdert Kennedy".[26] In a later edition of the book, Father Geoffrey himself adds a footnote about his call for Britain to be ruled by a government of unity with no political party interests and admits, "Recent happenings in England have made this passage sound absurdly optimistic."[27]

The criticisms were made over forty years after the First World War. When he voiced and penned his outspoken views, Father Geoffrey was in the midst of terrible battles in which thousands of British soldiers were slaughtered and in which he witnessed hundreds in wounded agony and lost count of the number he buried. Among them were young men he had known in Worcester and others he had got to know and respect in the short time he spent with them. In many cases, he sent letters to their mothers and wives. He had been stricken and almost died from gas attacks. The anger against Germans expressed in his words is not surprising.

There is another point about the book. In it he succeeded, at times, in communicating in the kind of working-class language familiar to many of the troops. He was less successful in presenting their views and opinions as voiced by them. A wounded officer asked him "What is God like?" and he attempted an answer.[28] He added that ordinary soldiers in the ranks asked the same question but "in the vast majority of cases, of course, it is not put in words because those who would ask it have no words to express it. It appears rather in the attitude of mind of these splendidly dumb soldiers who act and cannot speak."[29] As will be shown, Father Geoffrey does later convey their views, but in poetry rather than prose.

Some writers associated with the National Mission for Repentance and Hope did publish opinions very different from those of Father Geoffrey. In particular were those of George Lansbury, an Anglican Christian born in poverty, who had served the Labour Party and been an MP from 1910 to 1912. He was associated with the Mission, which appointed him as a member of one of its committees to plan the policies and practices of the church after the war. In 1916–17, he wrote a book called *Your Part in Poverty* with a preface by the Bishop of Winchester.

As a Christian pacifist, Lansbury opposed the war and claimed that many wealthy businessmen had welcomed it as a way of making money through the production of weapons and uniforms. By contrast, the wives and widows of ordinary soldiers were left with low incomes and he organized help for some of them in east London. He argued that poverty and gross inequality were contrary to the teachings of the Bible, and believed that reform would come through the working-class movement in general and the Labour Party in particular. He urged Christians to give both their support. Lansbury wanted the church as an institution "to take sides in the great moral issues involved in the social class war"[30] by backing the Labour Party.

Both Lansbury and Father Geoffrey wanted Britain to repent of its sins. Both longed for a revival with thousands turning to Christ. But whereas Lansbury wanted the church to side with working-class political movements, Father Geoffrey wanted to keep clear of political parties and believed that the church on its own could lead the way. Lansbury's short book did run to four publications in two years. But it received little publicity, blighted by his pacifism – at a time when conscientious objectors were very unpopular – by his distance from the front line and by his radical views on the redistribution of money and power. By contrast, Father Geoffrey had become famous as Woodbine Willie and, as a recipient of the Military Cross, was hailed as a national hero. His patriotism, his support for the war and his denunciation of Germany were all much more in tune with public opinion than were the views of Lansbury.

Father Geoffrey's book was written in a racier and more readable style than the measured sentences of Lansbury, and was enlivened by his descriptions of his own participation in battles. It was reprinted and reprinted. If Lansbury reached a few thousand readers, Father Geoffrey attracted tens of thousands.

# 5

# ROUGH RHYMES, 1917–18

*Rough Talks by a Padre* was not the only book that Father Geoffrey was writing in 1916–17 for publication in 1918. He was also composing poems or, as he modestly called them, rhymes. As he spent more time alongside ordinary soldiers, particularly in the trenches and under fire, so he heard and digested what they were saying and experiencing. In contrast to *Rough Talks*, he succeeds in expressing their words, thoughts, and feelings in a powerful manner, not in prose but in rhyme. He started writing them in 1916 but had not considered publishing them. However, a letter from Canon Frederick Macnutt to his church in Britain, dated 20 February 1917, shows how their publication happened. He too was a chaplain and met Father Geoffrey when they were conducting services in Boulogne for the National Mission for Repentance and Hope. Macnutt wrote:

> *[He] is one of the best Missioners I have ever known. He is an Irishman, as charming and as amusing and as eloquent as only an Irishman can be… I never knew anyone who had such power in getting the goods delivered as he gives his message to the men. One moment he has them in fits of laughter, the next he has hold of their heart-strings, and is drawing those hearts to Christ and all that is good. I feel I have learned a great deal from him, though I am an old hand at the job myself; and the way he gives the National Mission message is wonderful… One day I quoted some poetry to him, and he told me he did a bit at the poetry stunt and repeated some that he had written. They are as good as his addresses, and I suggested that he should write a poem for the men on the National Mission. Next day he brought me*

*the result and it was just what I wanted to read to the men.*
*After a bit of criticising and changing, it became A Sermon*
*in a Billet.*[1]

Macnutt was so impressed that he learned the poem by heart and several times recited it in public. Soldiers crowded around and asked where they could get a copy. He then informed Bishop Llewellyn Gwynne, the deputy chaplain general, about the rhymes. The bishop approved and sent them to the Society for the Propagation of the Gospels who arranged for publication by Hodder & Stoughton. They appeared in 1918 under the title *Rough Rhymes of a Padre*. It contained just thirty rhymes and was small enough to fit into a pocket. Many more rhymes were to follow.

"A Sermon in a Billet" is an example of Father Geoffrey using what he called dialect, the typical language of working-class soldiers, which showed their language, their thoughts, their judgements, their doubts, and their hopes. Later, various versions appeared and what follows is the one cited by Macnutt in his letter.

*Our Padre, 'e says I'm a sinner, and John Bull says I'm a saint,*
*And both of 'ems bun to be liars, for I'm neither of 'em, I ain't.*
*I'm a man, an' a man's a mixture, right from 'is very birth,*
*For part of 'im comes from 'eaven an' part of 'im comes from earth.*
*There's nothing in man that's perfect, and nothing that's all complete,*
*He's nobbut a big beginning from 'is 'ead to the soles of 'is feet.*
*There's summat as draws 'im uppards, an' summat as drags 'im down,*
*An' the consekence is 'e wobbles 'twixt muck an' a golden crown.*
*Ye remember ole Billy Buggins, the sargint what lost 'is stripes,*
*Well, 'e were a bloomin 'ero, a daisy to scrap but cripes,*
*That man was a blinkin' mixture o' all that were good an' bad,*
*'E broke 'is poor ole Mother's 'eart, the best friend ever 'e 'ad.*
*But 'e died to save a pal at Loos, an' that were the other side,*
*'E killed 'is Mother an' saved his pal, – that's 'ow he lived an' died.*
*Well, that's 'ow it is, it's 'uman, it's 'eaven an' earth in one,*
*There's an 'ell of a scrap in the 'eart o' man, an' that scrap's never done.*

*The good an' the bad's at war, ye see, the same as the boys an'*
*the Bosche,*
*An' when both gets at it wi' all their gans, there's a Saturday night*
*o' a squash,*
*An' it's just the same wi' the nations as it is wi' a single man,*
*There's 'eaven an' 'ell in their vitals a' scrappin as 'ard as they can.*
*An' England, she 'as it in 'er just same as all o' the rest,*
*Ole England's the same as us English men, a mixture o' bad an' best.*
*An' that's what I guess the parsons mean wi' their mission o'*
*pentance an' 'ope,*
*They want us to wash our country clean, wi' Jesus Christ for soap.*
*An' it ain't a bad stunt neither, for England oughter be clean,*
*For the sake o' the boys that's a fought an' died, an' the kiddies that*
*might 'a been.*
*We can't let it be for nuffin that our pals 'ave fought an' bled,*
*So, lads, let's look to the washin' up, for the sake o' Christ an'*
*our dead.*

He observed how soldiers adapted to months and years of killing and being killed and then conveyed their words and attitudes in his verses, particularly in "The Sniper":

*There's a Jerry over there, Sarge!*
*Can't you see 'is big square 'ead?*
*If 'e bobs it up again there,*
*I'll soon nail 'im – nail 'im dead.*
*Gimme up that pair o' glasses,*
*And just fix that blinkin' sight.*
*Gawd! that nearly almost got 'im.*
*There 'e is now – see? 'Arf right.*
*If 'e moves again I'll get 'im,*
*Take these glasses 'ere and see,*
*What's that? Got 'im through the 'ead Sarge?*
*Where's my blarsted cup o' tea?*

Yet even cynical soldiers longed for home. "Paradise" is a poem about how a soldier dreams of home. Father Geoffrey may well be putting into verse what a soldier has told him about his idea of paradise.

> *When machine-guns start to play*
> *At the ending of the day,*
> *And the sun's last burning ray*
> *Bleeds and dies.*
> *When the sable warp of night*
> *Is first cleft by silver light,*
> *With its sudden curving flight*
> *Of surprise.*
> *It is then that England calls*
> *From its cottages and halls,*
> *And we think of four dear walls*
> *And her eyes.*
> *When the children's prayer is said,*
> *And they lie tucked up in bed,*
> *And the fire is burning red –*
> *Paradise.*

Some soldiers just shrugged at the probability of death. Yet Father Geoffrey had knelt beside many dying men and in "To-day Thou shalt be with Me" he records how one did face it.

> *Gawd! 'ow it shoots!*
> *From my 'ead to my boots!*
> *And back to my 'ead again.*
> *You never can tell,*
> *But I don't think 'ell*
> *Can be worse than this blasted pain.*

> *There's 'eaven and 'ell,*
> *They say so, – Well,*
> *I dunnow what they mean.*

*But it's touch and go,*
*And I may soon know,*
*It's funny there's nothin' between.*

*I've drunk and I've swore,*
*And the girl next door*
*Is a' breakin' 'er 'eart thro' me.*
*She's a bonny lass –*
*Gawd damn this gas!*
*I wonder just where I'll be.*

*I remembers a day,*
*When they blazed away,*
*And they bust up a church to bits:*
*But the cross still stood,*
*It were only wood.*
*This pain – it's givin' me fits.*

*Ay, there it stands,*
*With its outstretched hands,*
*And I can't 'elp wonderin' why.*
*I can't quite see,*
*Is 'E lookin' at me?*
*O Gawd, am I goin' to die!*

*I can't! Not yet!*
*My Gawd, I sweat!*
*There's a mist comin' over my eyes,*
*Christ, let me be,*
*To-day with Thee.*
*You took a thief to Paradise!*

Father Geoffrey's compassion is not limited to soldiers. In "A Mother Understands", he attempts to feel like a mother who has lost a son and who also finds comfort in Christ:

*Dear Lord, I hold my hand to take*
*Thy Body, broken once for me,*
*Accept the Sacrifice I make,*
*My body, broken, Christ, for Thee.*

*His was my body, born of me,*
*Born of my bitter travail pain,*
*And it lies broken on the field,*
*Swept by the wind and the rain.*

Unusually, Father Geoffrey then adds a comment directly to Christ:

*Surely a Mother understands Thy thorn-crowned head,*
*The mystery of Thy piercèd hands – the Broken Bread.*

In his talks and prose, he warns soldiers against consorting with prostitutes. Yet his deep feeling and concern also extends to them in "A Gal of the Streets":

*I met 'er one night down in Leicester Square,*
*With paint on 'er lips and dye on 'er 'air,*
*With 'er fixed glad eye and 'er brazen stare, –*
*She were a gal on the streets.*

*I was done with leave – on my way to France,*
*To the ball of death and the devil's dance;*
*I was raving mad – and glad of the chance*
*To meet a girl on the streets.*

*I went with 'er 'ome – to the cursed game,*
*And we talked of men with the talk of shame;*
*I 'appened to mention a dead pal's name,*
*She were a gal on the streets.*

*"Your pal! Do you know 'im?" she stopped and said*
*"Ow is 'e? Where is 'e? I once knowed Ted."*
*I stuttered and stammered aht – "E's gorn – dead."*
*She were a gal on the streets.*

*She stood there and swayed like a drunken man,*
*And 'er face went green where 'er paint began,*
*Then she muttered, "My Gawd, I carn't"; and ran –*
*She were a gal on the streets.*

Father Geoffrey was just one of many poets who wrote during the First World War. Professor Malcolm Brown has written:

> *The Great War of 1914–18 is now seen as a supreme example of a literary war. Never was the poetry more searing, never was the prose more trenchant. The names of the most famous writers resound in the mind like members of a great brotherhood, Charles Hamilton Sorley, Edmund Blunden, Siegfried Sassoon, Robert Graves, Wilfred Owen, Edward Thomas.[2]*

Brown does not even mention Father Geoffrey. The great poets of the era wrote movingly, angrily, beautifully, powerfully, correctly. Father Geoffrey did not rank himself with them. Yet he was outstanding in a different way. Purcell, who cites several of Father Geoffrey's rhymes, comments:

> *No one would be likely to claim, and Geoffrey never did, any literary or artistic merit whatever for this kind of thing. But there is at least one reason why his verse in general and these early dialect poems in particular, is not lightly to be dismissed. It represents a break-through in the age-long problem of communication… No Church can go on indefinitely talking to itself.[3]*

Perhaps Purcell underestimates the literary merit of the rhymes. They move the emotions and stimulate the mind. However, it is true that their outstanding contribution is in the realm of communication. They not only convey the Christian message to working people, they also convey their thinking and believing to those who are usually socially distant from them.

Moreover, they were to be outstandingly popular. Father Geoffrey was encouraged to write more rhymes in response to public demand. *Rough Rhymes of a Padre* in 1918 was followed by *More Rough Rhymes of a Padre* in 1920. The same year saw the publication of *Peace Rhymes of a Padre*. *The Sorrows of God and Other Poems* came in 1921 and *Songs of Faith and Doubt* in 1922. *The Unutterable Beauty* was so successful in 1927 that nine reprints followed up to 1933. *Rhymes* appeared in 1929.

All these prints and reprints were for the future, however. Father Geoffrey was longing to be back on the front line. As Purcell puts it, "He was more than glad to claim from the Assistant Chaplain General the reward he had been promised… permission to return whence he had come."[4] Permission was granted.

# 6

# ON THE FRONT LINE AGAIN, 1917–18

By the middle of 1917, Father Geoffrey's wish had been granted. He was transferred to the 17th Brigade of 24th Division and was located near the Belgian town of Ypres. The town had already been the centre of earlier fighting because of its strategic importance, being close to a route to France. The Allies were keen to occupy it.

### The Messines–Wytschaete Ridge

The British and French armies planned a major breakthrough to take the strategically important town of Ypres. Before this could be achieved, the Messines–Wytschaete ridge, due south of Ypres, had to be taken. At 3.10 a.m., on 7 June, in a surprise attack, nineteen mines were detonated under the enemy lines. A military expert, J. H. Johnson, described it as: "The greatest earthquake ever felt in Northern Europe, accompanied by the mightiest crash ever heard by mortal man. Three great columns appeared out of the earth and rose slowly, majestically almost… For minutes, literally, falling debris, earth and stones rained down, and it was almost impossible to move."[1] The third battle of Ypres was under way.

The British troops did advance following the explosion until met by German machine gun fire from well-protected pillboxes. A further complication was continuous rain, with some men drowning in huge puddles. In 2011, the diary of one of the survivors was discovered in a Scottish loft. It belonged to Private Arthur Roberts who served with the King's Own Scottish Borderers and was one of the few black soldiers known to have belonged to a British regiment. He wrote, "We were shelled to blazes. I had a very narrow shave. One fellow in front of me had his head blown off. The chap beside him was severely wounded. I completely escaped. That was everyone around me was either killed or wounded."[2]

Father Geoffrey was at the ridge for the start of the battle. He later recorded that as he participated in the action, all kinds of thoughts ran through his mind. During the lulls, he wrote them down and they became the core of his book *The Hardest Part*, which will be discussed in the next chapter. Here some of his graphic observations and feelings are given.

> *I suppose it must be getting on time now. Five minutes past three, I make it, and ten minutes past is zero. It will be the devil of a shindy when it starts… God Almighty! What's that? It's the Hill gone up. Lord, what a noise! And all the earth is shaking. It must be like that Korah, Dathan, and Abiram business in the Book of Numbers up there. All the lot went down, women, children and all. I always thought it was hard luck on the children. It's like war though. War is just a mighty earthquake that swallows all before it. Now for it. Here come the guns. Listen to that big 12 inch. It sounds like a man with a loud voice and no brains in an argument. I thought I'd got the wind up and here I am laughing… That's the stuff to give 'em. It is a glorious sight, one silver sheet of leaping flame against the darkness of the trees. But it's damnable, it's a disgrace to civilisation. It's murder – wholesale murder. We can't see the other end – ugh – damn all war.*[3]

The signal was given to attack. He continued:

> *We're off now, over the top. I think I'm frightened. But that's bosh. I can't die. That's another thing I'm sure about. "Thanks be to God Who giveth us the victory through our Lord Jesus Christ." Anyway, I'm a skunk to think about that now. What does it matter if I do die?… except to her… and it is better for her and the boy for me to go out decent and respectable than to have to live on a beastly funk; so come on, you silly old fool, come on. Lord, that boy looks bad. Buck up,*

*lad, it will be alright. We've got 'em stiff... I say, damn all war, and those who make it! The kings and governors whose hearts God is supposed to turn and govern. Come on you chaps. That barrage is perfect. A cat couldn't live in it. Now we're well away. Lord what a howling wilderness the guns have made.*[4]

Father Geoffrey has made his first mention of his first son, Patrick, born a few days before the attack.

Father Geoffrey was given the task of locating a sheltered site for a first aid post for the wounded. He wrote soon after:

*It's about time to strike off to the left – on my own. There's the wood in which I've got to find a place for an Aid Post. It's been shelled pretty heavily. I believe I'm getting windy again... Good Lord, what's that? A dead Boche, I kicked him hard, poor little devil. He looks like a child that has cried itself to sleep. Here's the very place I'm looking for. It will make a splendid Aid Post. I wish it were not shelled so heavily.*[5]

With the post established and receiving casualties, Father Geoffrey went out to seek more wounded and to bury the dead. One of the killed was a sergeant he knew. Back at the post, he turned to the doctor: "This is the lot now, doc. The sergeant died so we did not bring him down. I'll bury him tomorrow... how that poor chap groans. All my togs are covered with his blood. Doc, I'm going to sleep. Call me in an hour."[6]

Just over a week later, it was the dawn of a day after a battle. Bringing in the wounded had gone on non-stop. He recorded, "I don't believe I could carry another one to save my life. I wonder – will that chap live? His thigh seemed all mash when we pulled him in. It was a beastly job. He cried for mercy and we had to drag him on just the same."[7]

As the troops advanced or retreated, Father Geoffrey went with them. He recorded later:

*In a German concrete shelter. Time 2.30 a.m. All night we had been making unsuccessful attempts to bring down some wounded men from the line. We could not get them through the shelling. One was blown to pieces as he lay on his stretcher.*

*I wonder how much this beastly shanty would stand. I guess it would come in on us with a direct hit, and it looks like getting some soon. Lord, that was near it. Here somebody, light that candle again. I wish we could get those chaps down. It was murder to attempt it though. That poor lad, all blown to bits – I wonder who he was. God, it's awful. The glory of war, what utter blather it all is.*[8]

After a short sleep, he woke up. "Doc, I've been dreaming. I'm going up to the line now. How's that lad inside? Dead? O God, comfort his mother. I must bury him at once. He was an only son."[9] He lamented over one he knew:

*On the last Sunday in June, 1917, the Advanced Dressing Station in which I was working was blown in and every one in it killed except the doctor, two stretcher cases, an R.A.M.C. sergeant, and myself. Among those killed was Roy Fergusson, my servant, a splendid lad of nineteen years, with whom I was great friends. He went out after the first shell had broken the end off the station to guide some walking wounded to a place of safety and was killed instantly. I found him leaning against a heap of sandbags, his head buried in his hands and a great hole in his back.*

*Poor old Roy. I thought I had saved his life when I sent him on that job. There seemed a decent chance of getting through and it looked a dead certainty that we should all be killed within a few minutes. There must have been a chance. All the walking wounded apparently got through, and he alone was killed. He probably warned them and took it himself. It would be like him. He looks as if he were saying his prayers. I must get the body carried across to the cemetery near Railway Dug-Outs and bury it at once. It will probably be unburied again before the morning if they start shelling again. That cemetery is an awful sight, with half the dead unburied; but it is the only place. His mother will surely want to know where he rests. Mothers always want to know that first.*[10]

He looked round for some soldiers to carry Roy's body to a grave.

*I say, you chaps, this lad was my servant. Could you help me across with him to the cemetery? You have to lift him very carefully, he's so badly shattered. That's the way. Now we'll carry him across and have the service while the lull is on. There is a grave ready. Would you mind staying while I say the service over him?*[11]

For weeks Father Geoffrey was engaged in saying the burial service in the mud. So were many other chaplains. But what happened next was unusual for a chaplain. He won the Military Cross. A full account of this incident, in his own words, was given in the opening pages of this book. Recapped in the words of his senior chaplain, the Reverend D. F. Carey, it was a dramatic incident:

*In one engagement the supply of morphine at a Dressing Station had run short, and he volunteered to fetch some from another Station. The ground he had to traverse was being heavily shelled, so that he had to run for short distances and then drop into shell holes for shelter. He successfully accomplished the task and returned to safety. He then volunteered to fetch in three wounded men, one of whom attempted to get in himself and was blown to pieces.*[12]

The official notice of the award was published in *The London Gazette* on 16 August 1917. It stated:

*For conspicuous gallantry and devotion to duty. He showed the greatest courage and disregard for his own safety in attending to the wounded under heavy fire. He searched shell holes for our own, and enemy wounded, assisting them to the Dressing Station, and his cheerfulness and endurance had a splendid effect upon all ranks in the front line trenches, which he constantly visited.*[13]

Interestingly, the announcement makes no reference to him obtaining the morphine yet does say that he assisted the enemy wounded to safety, which is not mentioned by those who have written about his bravery.

## Back Home

After the battle of Ypres, the war raged on. The British army was strengthened by the arrival of over 300 tanks and by the entry of the USA into the war. For the rest of 1917, no side could make a winning breakthrough. Father Geoffrey was no longer on the front line. The award of the Military Cross was accompanied by a bonus of ten days' leave. His stay in Britain – taken in August or September 1917 – may have been extended because of his asthma. Grundy refers to him "receiving treatment in a military hospital in Birmingham".[14] He must have been delighted at the opportunity to see not only Emily but also, for the first time, his son Patrick. Of course, he had already written to her about him and had sent her a poem called "To Patrick". It asks that the boy would receive the best not the worst of himself and ends with the following verse:

> *Fain would I give thee those bright wings*
> *On which my spirit flies,*
> *To talk with angels on the heights,*
> *In solemn sweet surprise,*
> *And win from Him, who is the Light,*
> *The poet's open eyes.*

It sounds as though he wants Patrick to be a poet like himself. Yet in a letter to Emily his advice on how to bring him up seems to desire a more athletic son. He wrote, "Make him a sportsman, encourage him to play games and play the game. Teach him to despise cowardice… Teach him that a gentleman should choose one of the poorly paid but honourable professions… teach him to love and reverence women."[15] His instructions are a reflection of one of the themes in his first book, *Rough Talks by a Padre,* that Christianity is to be equated with sport and sportsmanship.

Back in Worcester with his beloved Emily, Father Geoffrey experienced the thrill of seeing and holding Patrick. On the first Sunday, he preached at the morning service at St Paul's, addressed the children in the afternoon, and then baptized his son at the evening service in front of a packed church. On Monday, he visited children in the local school and, in the evening, met with a large number in the parish hall. His entry, wearing his medal, was greeted with applause. Sitting on a table he delivered a talk which was covered by the local paper. It read as follows:

> *Mr Kennedy was in his happiest vein, telling droll stories in his inimitable manner and describing graphically, with much pathos and humour, the many moving incidents which he has witnessed since his transference from the base to the fighting line. For more than an hour and a half, he held his large audience spellbound, and roars of laughter accompanied his many humorous allusions, while his more serious words were listened to with almost breathless eagerness. The vicar first explained why his "despatches" which he sent from time to time, and which were sometimes read from the pulpit, and at other times appeared in the press, ceased. His experiences were so awful, he hinted, that if he had written home about them, he would have frightened his wife and the congregation to death.[16]*

The report then covered Father Geoffrey's account of his frequent daily routine.

*At 7.30 he said matins in a little chapel in an old barn, and if he could get any communicants he celebrated as well. Then he wrote letters till 10 o'clock and, after that, he spent every day (except Sundays) from 11 to 6.30 in the lines. He took up a large box of Woodbines and some New Testaments, and marched round, sometimes talking about religion, and sometimes talking utter nonsense and playing the fool, but always giving away fags. "One of the best religious services we have", remarked the vicar, "is the one before a trench raid. We always have one and it is amusing to see the fellows in their tin hats, with their black faces and hands before a raid and they look just like a Christy minstrel troupe. I always go up with the men to a raid and that has tightened the bond between them and me enormously. If you get men into such a state that they will ask for a service, you have got hold of them. You must acquire the love of the men; be their comrade and friend."*[17]

Father Geoffrey was frank about his feelings towards the war.

*He said he was quite sure that they all felt as he did about the war – they were dead sick of the whole business. But they could not be half so sick of it as he was. What they said "out there" was that they were fed up and far from home… None of them were willing to give up until they had so completed this job that they had achieved the one object they had in view – that their children would never stand where they were standing. We could not destroy the German people – there were too many of them, and none of them hoped to complete the job by killing Germans. We wanted to destroy that mad megalomaniac Germany and put a sensible democratic Germany in its place.*[18]

He gave a brief and modest account of how he had won the Military Cross and added that he longed to be able to stay with them in Worcester. But he believed he should go back to the soldiers. He explained:

*"I want you to remember that while I am leaving you here it is not because I am not very earnest about the work here but because I believe the work I am doing out there is all-important"... In conclusion the vicar said that he was delighted with the way things had been going in the parish and he was grateful to them for the loyalty they had shown. It would have been an enormous grief to him if things had gone to pieces here. They ought to be more devoted to their religion and to their prayers than they ever were before because the soldiers needed their prayers very much and it helped them to know that they were praying for them at home.*[19]

## The Army Infantry Training Schools

If Father Geoffrey wanted to be back alongside the soldiers on the front line, he was disappointed. On returning to France he was chosen again to lecture to the troops. This time, instead of continually moving between numerous camps, he was charged with spending time at four Army Infantry Training Schools with the same brief at each: to raise morale and to present the Christian faith. This occupied his time from October 1917 to the early months of 1918.

The schools took about 400 officers and a similar number of non-commissioned officers for courses which lasted five weeks, after which they could expect a posting to the front. Initially, Father Geoffrey was located at No. 4 School at Flixecourt near Amiens, some thirty miles from the fighting. In a letter to his parishioners at St Paul's, he explained:

> *The General was keen that men should understand that Christianity was at the root of everything for which we fight and that a living faith was of the utmost importance in the conduct of the war, and for the conduct of that greater War of Reconstruction which must follow it.*[20]

Father Geoffrey was provided with a horse, had ample leisure time, and made many friends. In the letter, he admitted, "It is a soft job;

there is no use pretending otherwise, but I am glad of it, because it gives me not only a real opportunity to teach and reach, but a chance to train and get strong in preparation for harder work in the future."[21] In order not to be on the side lines, he joined the troops in their early morning exercises and in the lessons on self-defence and boxing. He must have smiled as he told his parishioners, "After a man has had the exquisite pleasure of punching a parson's nose, he is the more ready to listen to him preach."[22] Preach and lecture he certainly did, sometimes to the whole school, sometimes to smaller groups, and sometimes he organized lively debates. Following these, he would often mix with the men in the Church Army hut, which contained a canteen where he would talk, joke, and sing. The hut also doubled as the place for the Sunday services.

Just what did he talk and preach about? None of his addresses survive but in a letter to St Paul's, in between discussing what is happening in the church at home, he gives a mini sermon headed "The Failure of the Church". He states:

> There is enormous need of reform in the Church... We want to reform the Prayer Book and the lectionary and our forms of service, and our financial lack of system. We need to relieve bishops of absurd palaces and absurd incomes, and curates of absurd voices and affected mannerisms. We need more courage of conviction, and more honesty in witness to our truth, but with all her failings the Church is the purest and least corrupted department of national life still, and while she needs to humble herself before God, is not called to grovel before men... Never were thinking men so sure that Christ was right as they are now; never did men so long for brotherhood and lasting peace. Men once cried, "We have no king but Caesar" and now they cry from the ends of the earth, "We have no king but Christ, and as for Caesar let him be crucified. Now is our salvation nearer than when we believed." Churchmen, don't be downhearted, stand up to your critics; take from them all that is true, but throw their silly shallow lies in their teeth and bid them think.[23]

At this point, Father Geoffrey was confined to army circles and this summary is almost certainly from a talk he delivered to soldiers. It indicates his growing conviction that the church would have a leading role to play in post-war Britain. He calls upon troops to back the church both in war and peace. His address would have pleased the leaders of the National Mission for Repentance and Hope.

While at No. 4 School, Father Geoffrey met Colonel Ronald Campbell, who invited him to preach at his unit at Hardelot. Shortly before speaking, Father Geoffrey suffered an attack of asthma and had to rest. The same evening he attended a concert open to civilians as well as soldiers where his request to speak for ten minutes was granted. His talk gripped the audience and soon after, Campbell invited him to move to his school as chaplain. However, the colonel laid down the condition that there would be no compulsory parade services and, if men did not attend voluntarily, he would be sacked. Father Geoffrey gladly accepted and very soon he was holding three services, instead of the usual one, on Sunday mornings.

Campbell recorded:

> *He had a great influence for good with the men on my staff, which was reflected in their work. I took him with me to lecture at convalescent Depots, where he would speak to two or three thousand men, sometimes in the open air and sometimes at their meals. Never once did he fail to hold their attention and inspire them with the big things of life.*[24]

Campbell had a troupe – Father Geoffrey called it "the travelling circus" – which he took to troops in the field. It included Jimmy Driscoll, a former professional boxer, two champion wrestlers, and an NCO who had killed eighteen Germans with a bayonet. At the end of their display, during which he sometimes sparred with Driscoll, Father Geoffrey gave a twenty-minute talk, which always went down well. Campbell concluded, "I never met a man who was more fearless, both from a physical and moral standpoint. He would box anybody, he would ride any horse, and he could face any General who attempted to criticise him and his methods."[25]

In a letter to Emily, soon after he started at the training schools, Father Geoffrey wrote, "I will be able to get on with my book, and get it finished... here one is far away from the fighting and cannot even hear the guns."[26] The book he was referring to, published later that year, was *The Hardest Part*.

## To the Front Line – and Peace
Meanwhile, early in 1918, Germany took the offensive, broke through on the Somme, and came within forty miles of Paris. The Allies stood firm and contained the advance. By March 1918, Father Geoffrey could again hear the guns. He was transferred to the front line to join the 42nd Division. The German forces withdrew to what was called the Hindenburg Line, a network of barbed wire, trenches, and bunkers, which was difficult to overcome. Father Geoffrey was in the midst of the fighting and wrote a poem subtitled "On the Hindenburg Line, 1918" in which a soldier reflects on his experiences of suffering and of hope. Here the first and last of its six verses are given.

> *I've sung my songs of battlefields,*
> *Of sacrifice and pain,*
> *When all my soul was fain to sing*
> *Of sunshine and of rain.*

> *An exile in a weary land,*
> *My soul sighs for release,*
> *It wanders in war's wilderness,*
> *And cries for Peace – for Peace.*

The peace was getting nearer. The Allies, with great losses, did break through the Hindenburg Line and advanced towards Germany. Elsewhere the German navy mutinied while her allies, Austria and Turkey, accepted armistices. On 10 November, the Kaiser abdicated and the war ended on 11 November. The British prime minister,

David Lloyd George, announced in the Commons, "I hope we may say that thus, this fateful morning, came an end to all wars."[27] He regarded Britain as a victor, although the number of British and empire troops who died was nearly one million.

Unlike some other chaplains, Father Geoffrey did not have a quick return to Britain. He wrote in a letter to his parishioners, "I must tell you that the Bishop thinks that I had better remain with the army and sign on for another year."[28] He did not explain the reasons for this decision but he did indicate that he agreed with it. Monty Guiliford was another chaplain who stayed on. Brought up in a comfortable and financially secure family, he went to Cambridge University where he excelled more in sport than study. He became a priest in 1912 and, at the outbreak of war, he was married with one daughter. Like Father Geoffrey, he had not enlisted as a chaplain until the war was well under way, and it may well have been that those who joined in 1914 were released first. Many troops remained in France and Germany. Prisoners of war had to be guarded, vehicles and tanks repaired and made ready for transporting across the channel, camps had to be dismantled. These men still needed the services of chaplains. Guiliford's grandson, Peter Fiennes, reveals that he had duties in Belgium and Germany before "being home for good by the end of April, 1919".[29] Father Geoffrey did not see out the year he had expected and rejoined Emily and Patrick in March 1919.

## What Kind of Chaplain?

With his career as a chaplain coming to its end, it is appropriate to ask just what kind of chaplain he was. After all, by the end of the war there were 3,475 of them.

At the beginning of his discussion of the church at the front, Alan Wilkinson states, "The wartime ministry of the Church of England in general and the wartime ministry of Anglican chaplains in particular – both have had a bad press."[30] By press he means less the content of newspapers and more books written by former soldiers, nearly all officers. He draws on Robert Graves and writes, "Robert Graves' dismissive work of Anglican chaplains in *Goodbye*

*To All That* (first published in 1929) has been frequently quoted as the standard verdict... ordinary soldiers were in his opinion scornful of the Anglican chaplains."[31] C. E. Montague in his earlier and widely read *Disenchantment*, published in 1922, considered that Roman Catholic chaplains got closer to soldiers because they were more likely to come from working-class backgrounds. By contrast, he saw the Anglicans as bluff and jolly and asked, "had the parsons really nothing to say of their own about this noisome mess in which the good old world seemed to be floundering?"[32]

To be sure, there were ineffective chaplains who avoided the front line and could not communicate with ordinary soldiers. Others were a mixture who both kept a distance and got involved. Monty Guiliford had both a servant and a groom, which reflected his social standing. He did accompany troops to the front line but, once the fighting was over, he lived a separate life. A typical entry in his diary made on 10 November 1916 is as follows, "Glorious day. Bury Lieutenant K. Parsloe at Commercial City (Cemetery). Go over to Bertrancourt after lunch and take Morris and Clarke in (first class). Walk home to tea. Bridge. Write and bridge. Bed."[33] Meanwhile, ordinary soldiers were often confined to damp trenches with inferior food. On the other hand, Guiliford did join in football matches with them. Later he was awarded the Military Cross for "continuous bravery, self-sacrifice and devotion to duty". Like a number of other chaplains, his experience of war led him to abandon the Christian faith, although he subsequently regained it, became the leader of a youth club, and then a country parson.

This said, some Anglican parsons were outstanding. John Groser, a former radical priest in east London, made his presence felt when he knocked to the floor a drunken army medical officer who was singing bawdy songs. He preferred to be in the company of lower ranks in the trenches rather than in the officers' more comfortable quarters. In 1917, his unit suffered the deaths of over 200 men, leaving just 80 troops, the adjutant, the commanding officer, and Groser to cope with a German advance. The commanding officer divided the men into two groups, with the adjutant in charge of one and

Groser the other – a position he accepted providing that he was not required to kill. His commanding officer, Alan Hanbury-Sparrow, later recorded that Groser led with bravery and calmness.[34]

Another chaplain who worked hard for his men and who became almost as well known as Father Geoffrey was Philip (Tubby) Clayton. He rented a house and opened a club for fighting troops with a notice over the door, "Abandon rank all ye that enter here." Wilkinson comments, "After the trenches it seemed a home of love, warmth and vision."[35] On Easter Day 1916, ten celebrations of the Eucharist were held and soon afterwards the Archbishop of Canterbury, Randall Davidson, came to confirm thirty-seven men. After the war, Clayton founded the Toc H movement to serve ex-servicemen.

Whatever the view of Graves or others, being a chaplain could be dangerous and 172 chaplains (88 Anglicans) were killed or died as a result of the war. A number received decorations, with four receiving the Victoria Cross, the highest award for valour. Others received little recognition for their loyal service. One was the father of the Reverend Kenneth Woollcombe who, in 1997, gave a lecture in honour of Father Geoffrey. It started with a quotation from an unpublished letter from Woollcombe's father as he began being a chaplain in 1915. He was present at the first battle of the Somme when 60,000 British troops were killed or injured in one day. He wrote home:

> *The main ideas left in my mind now it's over are – indescribable noise, a ghastly redress, things hurtling through the air… The wailings of the wounded and the silence of the dead. I was terrified out of my seven senses and utterly overwhelmed and appalled. We went a good 24 hours without sitting down or taking food. Some of the wounds were too ghastly to describe. I thought I would swoon off many a time but I stuck it and slaved away with the doctors. I think my job was more in the first-aid line than in the parson's. They were most of them in far too great*

> *pain to grasp spiritual things but it was something like the*
> *work of Christ to hold a glass of water to a man cursing and*
> *blaspheming in his agony.*[36]

Like numerous other chaplains, he never received an award but he too was heroic.

Many chaplains were courageous. So was Father Geoffrey, but he also had other qualities which must rank him among the very best. He chose to spend as much time as possible alongside the ordinary soldiers. Whenever possible, he accompanied them when they left the trenches to go over the top. He worked in the makeshift hospitals and went out searching for the wounded. When he was off duty, he frequently made his way to the canteens, where he chatted, smoked, and sang with the troops. He sometimes joined them in their training and physical education. As already shown, there is no record of Father Geoffrey socializing with other officers. He devoted his time to the troops.

More than any other chaplain, he was prepared publicly to raise the questions which men were asking. Why does God allow war? How can a God of love ignore human suffering? What is the use of the church out here? He attempted to answer them and did not avoid the basic question: Does God even exist?

Certainly, he became the best-known chaplain among the soldiers. Purcell tells a much repeated story: "'Has Captain Kennedy come along?' an officer looking for Geoffrey once asked a sentry. 'No, Sir.' 'Have you seen the chaplain then?' 'No, Sir.' 'Look' said the officer, 'Have you seen Woodbine Willie lately?' 'Yes, Sir, just gone by.'"[37]

It was not just soldiers who got to know him or of him. In a way not matched by any other chaplains, his books were being read by a wide civilian audience. One title which had a huge impact was the book he was working on when he started at the training schools: *The Hardest Part.*

# 7

# *The Hardest Part,* 1918

As mentioned in the previous chapter, after the battles had ceased Father Geoffrey recorded the thoughts which came to him while in action. Some quotations were made from his vivid words. He further explained that the thoughts "fall into a kind of reasonable sequence".[1] Many of his thoughts became the core content of *The Hardest Part,* published in 1918, while the sequence allows six main themes to be identified.

## Disappointment with War

This contrasts with his earlier welcoming of the war and his positive expectations of what it would achieve. This change of tack is reflected in his introduction:

> *When they are old enough I am going to teach* The Hardest Part *to my sons, and I hope it will make them uncompromising and bitter rebels against the cruelty and folly and waste of war, and plant in their minds a strong healthy suspicion of the scheming, lying and greed that brings it about, and most of all that it will help to kill in their minds that power of sickly sentimentalism, that idiotic pomp and pageantry of militarism, which provide the glamour and romance for the mean and dirty shambles that are the battlefields of the world's great wars.*[2]

## Is God Almighty?

Next he tackles the big question of God's omnipotence. If he were so, then why does he allow wars? Father Geoffrey's answer is that God does not make his creatures into machines but gives them freedom of choice. They often choose violence and war. God's response is to suffer with humankind. As God the Son, he has entered into the world and suffered death on the cross. He knows what human emotional and physical pain is like. God is almighty but this is shown not in the abolition of war but in his love, which unites him with suffering men and women.

Father Geoffrey touched upon this theme in *Rough Talks by a Padre*. He now develops it by arguing that Christ not only suffered on the cross but also feels the pain of the victims of war. Just as a mother suffers when a son or daughter experiences suffering, so does God in Christ suffer when one of his creatures is in agony. It is just because Christ understands and feels pain that he is able to be alongside his followers through their terrible experiences. The suffering Christ becomes the ever-present Christ.

He also stresses that this theology is not just for soldiers. He says, "The Vision of the suffering God revealed in Jesus Christ, and the necessary truth of it, first began to dawn on me in the narrow streets and shadowed homes of an English slum. All that war has done is to batter the essential truth of it deeper, and cast a fiercer light upon the Cross."[3] As the war drew to a close, Father Geoffrey was preparing for his return home and the message he would take to his parishioners.

## The Centrality of the Sacraments

The Reverend D. F. Carey met with Father Geoffrey soon after the traumas at the Messines–Wytschaete ridge. He recorded that Father Geoffrey said to him, "You know this business has made me less cocksure of much of which I was cocksure before. On two points I am certain: Christ and His sacrament; apart from these I am not sure I am certain of anything."[4]

He was certain that Jesus Christ had shed his blood and had his body broken for the sake of humankind and he celebrated Communion most days. His war experiences then extended his understanding of the service. On the morning of 7 June 1917, he led a well-attended Communion service. He noticed a corporal who had come before and said over him the familiar words "Preserve thy body and soul into everlasting life." Sadly he had to write, "Three days later, I buried his body terribly mutilated in a shell hole just behind the line."[5] From his and other bodies he pondered over the meaning of their shedding of blood and breaking of bodies for others. He asked, "Is it wrong to see in them His Body and His Blood – God's Body and God's Blood? They are His; He is their Father, their Love and His Heart must bleed in them."[6] In other words, the sacrifices of men represented the sacrifices of God and this should be observed in the Communion service.

He also saw in the corporal a man who gave his life for a great cause in order to establish a better world. He mused that the usual Communion service attracted a core of regulars who had tended "to make the Sacrament an end itself rather than a means to an end, the great end of a Christ-like life".[7] The communicant comes to obtain personal forgiveness. Nothing wrong in that but it should also entail the desire to adopt a Christ-like life for the service of others, the great cause of social justice. We should be more like the corporal. He turns to the corporal again:

> *Goodbye corporal. I'll write to mother for you. Thank you for dying for me and teaching me so much. I will try to carry it out. The Church will, too. She is learning from the men that die. She will be more simple in the future. Christ is greater than the Church, and He can use her still, and through her revival He can save the world.*[8]

He thanks the corporal in the same way that he has frequently thanked the Christ.

## Prayer
Prayer is a common topic for books by Christian authors but few could be as challenging and unusual as Father Geoffrey. He starts in the trenches during heavy bombardment:

> *A sergeant on one side of me swore great oaths and made jokes by turns. A man somewhere on the other side kept praying.*

> *aloud in a broken and despairing kind of way, shivering out*
> *piteous supplications to God for protection and safety.*
>     *I wish that chap would chuck the praying. It turns me*
> *sick. I much rather that he swore like the sergeant.*[9]

Father Geoffrey argues that the soldier's prayer reflects the mistaken Christian notion that "prayer is a kind of magic cheque upon the bank of Heaven, only needing the formal endorsement with Christ's name to make it good for anything".[10] But these cheques are useless, he says. The millions of prayers for peace in 1914 were not effective. Parents and wives asked for the safety of loved ones, some of whom did survive but others died. He acknowledges, "I believe we parsons are to blame. We have not told people the truth about prayer for fear of hurting their feelings or discouraging them in their prayers."[11]

So what is the truth? He turns to Christ who, when in Gethsemane, asks that the torture and death on the cross should not come about. Father Geoffrey explains:

> *This is not His prayer, that is what He is praying against,*
> *that is the expression of the terror He has to fight. But each*
> *time the prayer follows, the real prayer, with power that is*
> *immediately answered. The angel of God appears to comfort*
> *Him. Terror dies within His soul, hesitation disappears, and*
> *with His battle prayer upon His lips, "Thy will be done,"*
> *He goes out from the garden in the majesty of manhood to*
> *bear such witness to His truth, to live in death so fine a life,*
> *that He becomes the light in darkness of every age, and the*
> *deathless hope of a dying world.*[12]

Real prayer is the prayer not for safety but for courage to do God's will. He says, "The first prayer I want my son to learn to say for me is not 'God, keep daddy safe.' But 'God, make daddy brave, and if he has hard things to do make him strong to do them.' Life and death don't matter."[13] He explains:

*As God did not quench the fires that burned the martyrs or close the lions' mouths before they tore them limb from limb, so God does not turn aside the shell that flies shrieking out the call to martyrdom for me or for my son... Christ never promised to those who prayed immunity from suffering and death.*[14]

His definition of prayer is "the means of communication by which the suffering and triumphant God meets His band of volunteers and pours His spirit into them, and sends them out to fight, to suffer, and to conquer in the end."[15]

## Love of Nature

The fifth theme is his love of nature. Father Geoffrey felt near to God in the peaceful surroundings of nature. His brother Gerald, recalling their walks in the country as young men, said, "I have never known any man to whom the beauty of nature spoke so vividly and directly of God... he would stand still and silently enjoy the beauty of a scene."[16] Away from the peace and in the midst of war, he could still identify the beauty of nature. While in a shell hole, he observed, "What a perfect morning it is. All the sky burns red with the after-blush of dawn, and here I seem surrounded by a soft grey sea of mist. What unutterable beauty there is in nature... I suppose the first of all God's fruits by which we may know Him is the world of nature."[17]

Father Geoffrey believed that God was revealed in the colours and peace of nature. Ever realistic, he also noted another side to nature and identified "snakes and earthquakes, volcanoes, plagues and floods... the lamb and the lion do not lie down together but are at war".[18] Good and evil coexist in God's world and God "calls us to join Him in the task of conquering the evils which arise from the necessities of creation. He calls us to combat famines and pestilence and disease."[19]

Father Geoffrey returns in his thoughts to the burial of one of the wounded who did not recover. As he digs he thinks:

*Good old earth, what would I do without you? Poor old patient mother earth, with all your beauty battered into barrenness by man's insanity. He who made you is not dead, though crucified afresh. Some day He will rise again for you, and all this wilderness that man has made will blossom like the rose, and this valley will laugh with laughter of summer woods and golden grain, and cottage homes in whose bright gardens children play at peace and unafraid.*[20]

This is Father Geoffrey at his best in his ability to bring hope out of sadness. He starts with the soil being used to conceal a victim of man's cruelty to man. Then he perceives how from the same soil will emerge the beauty of nature and the same battlefield will become a haven for children.

## Learning from the Ranks

The sixth theme is not so much a theme as an approach in which Father Geoffrey accepts the contribution of ordinary soldiers. In *Rough Talks by a Padre*, he revealed how he could talk to working-class troops. There was less evidence in it that he learned from them. This changed as he spent more time with them on the front line, as he depended upon their abilities and heard their views.

Perhaps surprisingly for an Anglican clergyman, he now understands and passes on – in his new book – the coolness of many soldiers towards the monarchy. After a big battle, the men were put on parade to receive the thanks of their commander and it finished with the singing of "God save the King". Father Geoffrey comments:

*The divine right of kings is an idea as foreign to the British soldier's mind as the infallibility of the Pope. To him it is purely a matter of expediency whether you have a king with a crown or president with a top hat... The pomp and pageantry of kings, the glamour that surrounds a throne, the outward symbols of royalty have lost all power of appeal to*

*the ordinary man… The sentiment of passionate loyalty to the*
*king does not exist among the rank and file of the army.*[21]

Instead they want democracy:

*Everywhere I find among the men of the army that this is*
*the one thing that touches them and rouses real enthusiasm.*
*They do believe in democracy… They believe intensely that*
*every man has a right to a voice in the government of his*
*country. This conviction is the only one of an ultimate kind*
*that I find common and intense throughout the British*
*Army. If they have any religion, it is centred in this idea of*
*Democratic freedom.*[22]

It must be added that a few pages later he writes that he admires
the king and that "if any king survives it will be ours, for he is very
nearly a Christian king".[23] Nonetheless, he insists that ordinary
soldiers are democrats before they are royalists.

He then moves on to express the opposition of working-class
soldiers to the hierarchical nature of British society. This society is
dominated by those of high birth, privileged education, and wealth,
yet the men have discovered that what counts in battle is the
courage and abilities of those who may lack all these advantages.
Father Geoffrey agrees.

*No superiority of breeding or of brains, no pre-eminence of*
*social position, no power of wealth, appeals to us apart from*
*service. An idle duke is frankly disreputable, and infinitely*
*inferior to a working dustman. The dustman may perhaps*
*die a pauper, but that is nothing to the disgrace of living as*
*a parasite.*[24]

Father Geoffrey acknowledges that in ordinary soldiers he sees and
learns about Christ. He declares:

*All men are learning to worship patient, suffering love, and
the muddy bloody hero of the trenches is showing us Who is
the real King. The darkness is clearing away, and men at last
are growing proud of the cross. Beside the wounded tattered
soldier who totters down to this dressing-station with one
arm hanging loose, an earthly king in all his glory looks
paltry and absurd. I know nothing in real religion of the
Almighty God of power. I only see God in Christ, and these
men have shown me –* Him.[25]

Not least, Father Geoffrey agrees fully with those soldiers who
demand that, in post-war Britain, poverty must be abolished. He
has no hesitation in attacking the church for upholding the social
structure of "The rich man in his castle, The poor man at his gate".[26]
He almost shouts, "It makes a man who has studied modern poverty
mad with rage to be told that Christ blessed the poor, and said they
would always be with us."[27] He calls for a society in which there
will be no more poor people.

Purcell wrote about this book in 1962, "... while it came out
of the war, it outlasted the war. It was being re-printed seven years
afterwards, and is quoted to this day."[28] In *The Hardest Part*, Father
Geoffrey graphically describes the excitement and horror of war,
considers the theological questions it provokes, and identifies the
new society envisaged by soldiers. It is readable and challenging,
straightforward yet profound. It is probably his best book. And
while it was being widely read in Britain, Father Geoffrey returned
to his country considering how the lessons of war would shape his
priesthood in Worcester.

# 8

# From Local Priest to National Preacher, 1919–21

On 21 March 1919, Father Geoffrey disembarked at Folkestone and made his way to Worcester, to St Paul's, and to his family. He was still a priest devoted to his parish, still a loving husband and father. He was still generous to the needy, still full of laughter, and still liable to asthma.

A few years later, in 1924, he toured the USA and Canada to address thousands of people. In Toronto, he filled the Convocation Hall, with many others being unable to get in. Fortunately, the talk was broadcast on one of the new radio programmes. His topics were national and international, dealing with the cynicism produced by the war and the need to reconstruct education. Above all, as reported in the press, "His real mission is to the poor and outcast."[1]

From being a priest in a small parish, he had become the chief speaker for a national organization and was in demand as a famous speaker all over Britain and beyond. How did the transformation occur? The answers are to be found both in the changes – or lack of changes – in the conditions of Britain, and also in Father Geoffrey himself.

## St Paul's, the Same Yet Different
Back home in the rectory, Father Geoffrey enjoyed the daily company of Emily and Patrick. His wife was again his help-meet, his fellow worker at the church and in the parish. She also protected him and tried to ensure that he took more rest at home. Home was his delight. A few months after he arrived back, he wrote:

> *It is very peaceful. There is a bowl of roses on my study table. My child is playing on the patch of garden outside. I can hear*

*my wife calling him, and his gleeful little voice chuckling as*
*he runs away to hide. I have just had tea. It is peace. I can*
*feel the old life creeping round me, calling me.*[2]

As the parish priest, he again gave priority to conducting worship
in the church with the sacrament celebrated nearly every morning.
On Sundays, services took place in the morning and evening, and
were well attended. In the afternoon, the Sunday school met with
Emily as one of the leaders. Father Geoffrey wanted more than
worship for his people and in 1921 a new Church Army Social
Centre was opened. He frequently visited his parishioners. One
woman recorded that he "probably converted more people over
pints of beer than anywhere else".[3]

Father Geoffrey was popular with the children, yet one man
remembered that he could be sharp with them: "Stern, strict and
abrupt with those who failed to attend church and sending choirboys
home if their shoes were dirty."[4] But his kindness outweighed his
strictness. Another woman recalled:

*I remember with joy when he arranged for me – the only child*
*present – to sit in front of the dress circle at the Theatre Royal*
*when he addressed a huge audience of working men. At the*
*end, they all sang* When I Survey the Wondrous Cross. *The*
*experience has remained vividly with me all my life and I*
*cannot hear that hymn without the tears flowing.*[5]

His generosity was ever in evidence with a readiness to give his
clothes and other possessions to those in need. His forgetfulness
had not changed. For a while he drove around in a small Morris
car, omitted to obtain the five shillings driving licence, and was
taken to court.

Above all, his heart went out to those in poverty. As one of
his former parishioners explained, he was "a poor people's parson
who was so humble and so earnest".[6] To his disappointment, the
outcome of the war was to increase rather than decrease the extent

of material want. The parish now contained numbers of widows whose wage-earning husbands had been killed. These lone parents often had several children. Others lost the love – and the incomes – of their sons. In other cases, husbands survived but were unable to work because of terrible injuries. Father Geoffrey's feelings were expressed in one of his best poems, thought to be based on a couple he knew. "The Pensioner", as it is called, is about a woman who recalls her happy life with a loving, hard-working husband before the war. Then she describes her present experiences with her badly injured man. It is not lack of money that hurts her but the fact that war has ruined their former relationship.

> *Look ye what the war's done at 'im*
> *Lying there as still as death.*
> *See 'is mouth all screwed and twisted,*
> *With the pain of drawing breath!*
> *But of course I 'ave a pension,*
> *Coming reg'lar ev'ry week.*
> *So I ain't got much to grouse at –*
> *I suppose it's like my cheek,*
> *Grousin' when a grateful country*
> *Buys my food and pays my rent.*
> *I should be most 'umbly grateful*
> *That my John was one as went,*
> *Went to fight for King and Country,*
> *Like a 'ero and a man,*
> *I should be most 'umbly grateful,*
> *And just do as best I can.*
> *But my pension won't buy kisses,*
> *An' 'e'll never kiss again,*
> *'E ain't got no kissing in 'im,*
> *Ain't got nothing now – but pain.*
> *Not as I would ever change 'im*
> *For the strongest man alive.*
> *While the breath is in my body*

*Still I'll mother 'im – and strive*
*That I keeps my face still smiling,*
*Though my heart is fit to break;*
*As I live a married widow,*
*So I'll live on for 'is sake.*
*But I says – let them as makes 'em*
*Fight their wars and mourn their dead,*
*Let their women sleep for ever*
*In a loveless, childless bed.*
*No – I know – it ain't right talkin',*
*But there's times as I am wild.*
*Gawd! You dunno how I wants it –*
*'Ow I wants – a child – 'is child.*

Father Geoffrey realized that the straits of people like this couple were not confined to St Paul's. His mixing with many soldiers abroad showed him that poverty was a national problem. At the same time, his daily contact with former soldiers and their families kept the memory of the war alive within him. So much so that he brought about the erection of a memorial crucifix outside the south end of the church where it stands to this day. It was constructed by a skilled sculptor, George Sprague, to Father Geoffrey's own design. Unusually, and to some controversy, Christ's head was not hanging in agony but was erect, even defiant. It stood on a six-foot base made from Portland stone on which were engraved the names of 140 Worcester men killed in the war.

On 10 April 1921, in front of a huge crowd, it was unveiled by Emily Studdert Kennedy who, in a moving speech, said:

*I unveil this memorial Calvary to the men who died for us*
*in the Great War – doing it not in my own person – but as*
*representative of the mothers of this parish who gave their*
*sons and the wives who gave their husbands and I pray from*
*the bottom of my heart God may comfort them and grant to*
*these their loved ones Light and Rest. How you love your*

*dear ones. I may love your dear ones because love only is eternal – your dear ones bear your love in their hearts up to the tenderest heart of all. We have no such word as death except for those things which ought to die. For us, death has no more dominion because Love Himself has triumphed, and has won the victory.*[7]

Father Geoffrey Kennedy then delivered an address which is worth repeating in full:

*I hope that for ever and ever the memorial will have a message for the people of St Paul's and their children. They will find here written on the stone, "To the memory of the men who gave their lives" – not for their country. I have not written that. I have written "who gave their lives for us." I have not said that they died for their country because to say that would have been to say at once too much and too little. It was something much larger than their country for which they died, and at the same time it was something very much more intimate and smaller.*

*I often asked men at the front what they were fighting for, and generally they would take out from their pocket a photograph of a woman and two or three children, and say "That is what I am fighting for" – and that was the little intimate, dear and tender thing for which these men fought and died. Rightly or wrongly they were led to believe that it was the call of God, and they gave their lives to defend their wives and their little ones. It was for these little causes that they died, and so I have written on the stone "for us."*

*It would be too small a thing to say that they died for their country, because when I say they died for us I not only mean that they died for their wives and children and their country, but they died, as I believe they did, for the whole wide world. They died the best of them, in the last moment of their lives, believing that by their death they were bringing nearer the days when wars will cease and peace shall reign. So far it seems that their sacrifice has not borne much fruit, but whether it bore fruit or not takes nothing away from the nobility of that sacrifice.*

*With regard to the figure on the Cross, it is a message to us all. It is not the same as the figure on some crucifixes. The Christ has His head held erect. He was not beaten, broken or defeated. They took His body and broke it, and hung it between the earth and sky, but His spirit was unbroken and so was the spirit of your brothers and fathers who died unbroken and unbeaten. Tell your children that the crucifix means the victory of good over evil. I could not bring myself to have a Calvary made where Christ looked broken and dead. In depicting Him as he has done I think that Mr Sprague, the artist, has preached to us an everlasting sermon in wood. I pray that it will stand with its message, warning people that they must never forget. People are forgetting the war and I cannot blame them altogether, but we must not forget the lessons we ought to have learned from it. Take that message home, and remember to keep the message of it ever green.*[8]

## Politics and Disillusionment: "The Same Old World"

So much for the small parish of St Paul's. What was happening in Britain as a whole? The end of the war in 1918 was followed by a general election in December in which, as a result of electoral reforms, six million women and three million men were able to vote for the first time. The outcome was that David Lloyd George continued as prime minister of a coalition government made up of Conservatives and some Liberals. It promised a land "fit for heroes".

Initially many returning troops found jobs, often with their former employers. Then the end of wartime controls on profits and prices led to rising costs for the public. Unemployment set in as more soldiers were discharged, so that by November 1919, 350,000 former soldiers were out of work. Particularly vulnerable were those who had sustained serious injuries. Next, the wartime demand for British coal, steel, and textiles declined. By the end of 1921, unemployment had climbed to two million. The situation was made worse by a severe shortage of housing. There were few homes for heroes. Kerry Walters, an American professor of peace and justice studies at Gettysburg College, has published an anthology of Father Geoffrey's writings. He commented of this period, "The government seemed reluctant to tackle the very real problems such as class privilege and poverty. Business men who had profited from the war grew richer, and disabled veterans and war orphans and widows grew poorer. It was the same old world."[9]

It is true that the government did make some response. It extended the coverage of unemployment pay so that the existing fifteen shillings a week was given for two sixteen-week periods with a gap in between. The Labour Party condemned the amount as too small and pointed out that in the gap the men still had to turn to the unpopular Poor Law. Another drawback was that the increased payments were met by reducing expenditure on educational and health services. Some public anger was expressed in marches of protest, and in October 1921 police made a baton charge on a huge demonstration in Trafalgar Square. C. E. Montague, a former soldier, wrote bitterly about politicians who had promised a better Britain yet delivered "more poverty, less liberty, more likelihood of other wars, more spite between masters and men, less national comradeship".[10]

The lack of public trust spread beyond politics. C. E. Montague's book was aptly entitled *Disenchantment*. He had been disgusted at the conduct of the war and told how senior officers had forced troops to advance into an obvious ambush where they were mown down by machine gun fire. He had lost confidence in the press – and he was a former journalist – which printed misleading accounts of battles and subsequently praised politicians who failed to tackle mass unemployment. He wrote, "Respect for the truthfulness of the press was clean gone."[11] He perceived a national disenchantment which led to apathy and an acceptance of vast inequalities.

Disenchantment also bred cynicism. Purcell noted, "The early twenties were strange times: embittered, disillusioned, poisoned by a sense of anti-climax so absolute that the only possible answer, among thinking people at any rate, seemed to be one of all pervading cynicism."[12] Richard Overy, in his book *The Morbid Age,* identifies this cynicism in the literature of the time and he quotes the famous medical missionary and organist, Albert Schweitzer, who in a public lecture declared: "It is now clear to everyone that the suicide of civilisation is in progress."[13] Father Geoffrey, as he makes clear in his books being published at this time – which will be discussed later – was troubled by the prevailing moods of disillusionment and cynicism. When designing the crucifix of Christ at St Paul's, he insisted on a Christ not hanging in despair but in expectancy. He wanted to proclaim a gospel with a positive message of hope and justice for society. The question was whether the church as a whole was ready and equipped to do the same.

## The Unchanged Church

The war, for all its expected heartbreaks for those whose loved ones would die, prompted two hopes, even expectations, within the Church of England and probably in other churches as well. One was that, as its chaplains would serve many ordinary soldiers, so they would develop the skills to communicate with them. On their return to Britain after the war, they would teach others how to reach working-class people and so make the church less dominated by the middle class. The other hope was that the war with all its dangers would make citizens and soldiers turn to God. Post-war this could develop as a religious revival.

The church initiated the National Mission for Repentance and Hope as a vehicle for these intentions in Britain and among the troops. Certainly, as already shown, Father Geoffrey did succeed in communicating to all social classes and did get positive responses from soldiers. But he – and a few colleagues – was the exception. Donald Hankey was from a rich family but his strong Christianity and his desire to reach ordinary soldiers with the gospel led him to enlist as a private. He acknowledged that, on the front, there were well-intentioned chaplains, some mixed with other ranks, several showed great bravery. But few, in his opinion, were adept at relating verbally and emotionally with the other ranks. Hankey was killed on the Somme in October 1916. After his death, some of his writings were published in *The Spectator* magazine and later as a book. He recorded that he longed to talk Christianity with his fellow troops but found it difficult because the middle and working classes spoke in different ways and used different words and concepts. He added that the soldiers should not be blamed, and admitted, "It is certainly arguable that we educated Christians are in our way almost as inarticulate as the uneducated whom we want to instruct."[14]

Post-war developments within the church were little better. Wilkinson brought together evidence to show that just as no religious revival occurred within the war, nor did one take place afterwards. The Church of England remained essentially middle class. The explanation, he argued, was partly that "the ordained leadership of the Church of England was not involved in the actual experiences of work in an industrial society".[15] The lifestyle of the clergy, their language and thought processes, their lack of experience in industrial work, the kind of friends they made, and the leisure activities they pursued were very different from those who laboured long hours with their hands, often in very unpleasant conditions. Not surprisingly, the two classes found it difficult to communicate and were not comfortable in each other's company.

Far from revival and growth, the indications were of a downward spiritual spiral. The post-war years saw a shortage of men applying to be ordained. In 1919, it fell to 161. To his credit, the Archbishop of Canterbury, Randall Davidson, took the initiative and sought recruits from men leaving the armed forces and set aside £378,000 to finance their training. Over the next three years 675 were trained ,of whom 435 were ordained. However, by 1924 nearly all were in post and the annual intake of ordinands became smaller than the number of clergy retiring or dying.

Some church leaders were aware of and very concerned about the problems. The National Mission for Repentance and Hope set up five committees of inquiry whose reports were published in 1919. All made some impact. The first confirmed that the church was still out of touch with working-class people. The second contributed to a revision of the Prayer Book. The third recognized that many people found the growing labour movements more inspiring than the church. The fourth complained that the church did not govern itself and was too subject to parliament. The fifth called for changes in the system of industrialization. It claimed that the huge size of industrial companies had lessened contact and harmed relationships between owners and workers so reducing the position of the latter to "hands" with little security of employment.

The reports drew fierce criticisms from conservative clergy and church members but won the support of more radical elements. Among the latter were the Reverend William Temple and the Reverend Dick Sheppard. Both were well known within Church of England circles. Temple, the son of an Archbishop of Canterbury, had risen rapidly up the ecclesiastical hierarchy and by 1919 was Canon of Westminster. Sheppard, the son of a prominent cleric close to Queen Victoria, was vicar of the famous St Martin-in-the-Fields Church in central London. Fully involved in the National Mission for Repentance and Hope, Temple had contributed to the foundation of the Life and Liberty Movement as a kind of ginger group for church reforms. Sheppard also gave his support. It criticized the anomalies in church pay, with some vicars in rural parishes receiving £2,000 a year while those in overcrowded slum parishes might get £400. It played a leading part in persuading politicians to pass the Enabling Act in 1919, which allowed the Church of England to set up elected bodies, containing lay representatives, to shape certain church policies. Both Temple and Sheppard admired Father Geoffrey, befriended him, and drew him into the Life and Liberty Movement. Before long, he was participating in their meetings. These were largely organized by Temple all over England. The movement wanted the Church of England to be less dominated by parliament, which could still block changes to the Prayer Book. It pushed for much greater involvement of the laity in decisions about church organization and policy.

Father Geoffrey believed that the teachings of Jesus Christ contained the values and practices which should underpin society. The need to ensure no more war, to show the evil of poverty and to counter the disenchantment within the country could be fulfilled by a more Christian population. He acknowledged that the church had failed to convey this message to many in the community. Temple and Sheppard – along with others – were reinforcing his belief that he could convey a message to large audiences, especially working-class ones. They encouraged him to broaden his speaking horizons.

## Changes in Father Geoffrey

Father Geoffrey might not have accepted invitations to speak all over the country – and indeed might not have received them – but for two other factors. One was that he had become a figure known to many thousands in Britain. His role as the effective and brave Woodbine Willie had spread not only through the church but also through the civilian population. His books, especially his rhymes, were widely read and quoted. Not least, on 17 May 1920, he was invited to be a chaplain to King George V. He did not hesitate to accept and thereafter preached at least twice a year at services which the king attended. He became famous, and his fame both boosted his confidence in his own speaking abilities and also stimulated churches and other institutions to press him to speak to their members.

There was another factor. Ever since his days at theological college, his ability to preach had been noticed. But by 1919 there was a vehemence in his opinions and in the way he delivered them. His opposition to war makes the point. The Dean of Worcester, William Moore Ede, observed, "He became convinced that war is an unmitigated evil."[16] An initial supporter of Britain's participation in the war, he expressed his change of view in his brilliant poem called "Waste".

*Waste of Muscle, waste of Brain,*
*Waste of Patience, waste of Pain,*
*Waste of Manhood, waste of Health,*
*Waste of Beauty, waste of Wealth,*

*Waste of Blood, waste of Tears,*
*Waste of Youth's most precious years,*
*Waste of ways the Saints have trod,*
*Waste of Glory, waste of God, –*
*War!*

The same passion was conveyed whenever he spoke, and his zeal and sincerity gripped audiences.

## Speaker in Demand

Once settled back at St Paul's, Father Geoffrey was ready to respond to a growing number of invitations to address meetings. He left no notes of his talks and, of course, tape recorders did not exist. But parts of his talks were reproduced in his books and the local and national press and, especially, church papers gave coverage of some of them.

One of his first invitations was in 1920 to Wellingborough, where he knew the vicar of the parish church. On the Sunday morning, the 1st Northants Regiment assembled in the Market Square and, accompanied by massed bands, marched to All Saints' Church. Father Geoffrey preached at the service and, according to a report in the local paper, he declared "that the only way to secure a permanent peace was by bringing about a change to men's hearts and minds".[17]

In the afternoon, a men's service was held where he stated that "the world was infinitely worse today than ever in the history of the world before".[18] He made an outspoken attack on the Peace Conference, dominated by the victors of the war, and predicted that the forcing upon Germany of heavy financial demands and restrictions on their right to future re-armament would lead to further conflict. The paper reported that he closed "by asking the men to take a clean and intelligent grasp of things and to keep themselves pure".[19]

At evensong, he preached again and the paper explained that he gave a "telling discourse from the first words of the Creed, I believe in God. Every man, he said, had a God and a creed of some sort, Venus, Bacchus or Christ."[20]

On 11 February, *The Church Times* gave coverage of his address in York under the heading "Remarkable sermon in York Minster". He focused on global problems, particularly the thousands dying of hunger. He argued: "What is needed is the combined efforts of all men of goodwill to wrest from nature the food and wealth that is there in such abundance."[21] The reporter summed up, "It was a brilliant sermon, plentifully relieved by flashes of humour and quick blows straight from the shoulder, but in depth and constructive thought making a very distinctive advance in the development of this modern prophet."[22]

These talks – in a local parish church and then in one of the country's foremost Christian institutions – focused on individual responsibilities and actions more than politics. Soon after, he participated in a meeting organized by the Life and Liberty Movement at Queen's Hall in London which was more overtly political. Other speakers included Cosmo Lang, the Archbishop of York, Maude Royden, a feminist, socialist, and lay preacher, and Ernest Bevin, leader of the Dockers' Union and supporter of the Labour Party. Bevin called upon the church to march with Labour. A report in *The Church Times*, headed "Speech on the Labour Party. Class Hatred A Great Obstacle to Progress", dwelt on what Father Geoffrey said in reply: "For God's sake, let the Church join hands with Labour and together march against the curse of war."[23] The reporter then added, "Studdert Kennedy declared himself in favour of nationalisation of some departments but did not believe it to be a panacea for every evil."[24] He then warned that the church had to be distinct from the Labour Party and, turning to Bevin, declared that "one of the greatest obstacles between us... was the class hatred created by the Labour Party... the real movement towards better things was due to the union of men from all classes".[25] He added "that in his opinion the Church, if she went hand-in-hand with the Labour Party, would make one of the greatest mistakes in her history".[26]

His speech was important in revealing the direction of his thought. He showed some sympathy towards the Labour Party but did not want to be a part of it. In this, he disagreed with a number of Christian socialists who were both strong Anglicans and members of Labour. He argued that social reform was more likely to come from unity between people of different classes.

On Good Friday 1921, he spoke at a packed meeting at the Strand Theatre in London. A report in a church paper was headed "The Bravery of Christ. Good Friday Sermon Spellbinds A Vast Crowd. Woodbine Willie. Men And Women In Tears".[27] He spoke for three hours with breaks for hymns. The reporter wrote that the crowd "sat as if hypnotised, thrilled, moved often to tears, held prisoner by the eloquence of the man whose soul was on fire".[28]

In this Good Friday talk, Father Geoffrey did not dwell upon the case for peace or social reform. He focused on the life and death of Christ and, in particular, on his bravery. His courage on the cross had been central to his design of the crucifix at St Paul's. Now he enlarged on this as a characteristic shown throughout Christ's life. He called upon Christians to be like Christ, to be brave in the face of opposition, to be proud rather than ashamed of their faith. In his conclusion, the reporter said:

> He uttered a new point of view on God's relation with men. "God has no enemies," he said quietly and feelingly. "You may hit God, but He will never hit you. God's love is like that of a mother for her beautiful child who has a filthy skin disease. He loves the dirtiest, meanest scum of a man who will go home tonight and beat his wife as much as He loves you or me"... "A mother's love," he said in a whisper, "can make a child's sin, her sin; his shame, her shame; his grief, her

*grief." He paused: then his voice thrilled out with – "God is*
*a mother's love ad infinitum."*[29]

These talks demonstrate that as a Christian he was concerned about
social problems and injustices. But this does not mean he was no longer
preaching about the way in which God wants to transform individuals
and draw them into a loyal and loving relationship with himself.

## *Lies*

On top of all his other activities, Father Geoffrey managed to write
three new books in this period. How did he do it? A journalist with
one of the Worcester papers offered to help. He wrote:

> *There followed many pleasurable evenings together – most of*
> *my duty free time being spent at St Paul's vicarage. Studdert*
> *Kennedy was doing a series of articles which he subsequently*
> *published as* Lies. *He would dictate at tremendous speed,*
> *smoke and choke; then, if he had not made his meaning*
> *thoroughly clear, he would scrap it all and start again.*[30]

The journalist took it down in shorthand and later typed the pages.

The book was written and published in 1919. It consisted of fifteen
chapters, all of which deal with a common lie. Three of the lies, those
which distort the truth of nature, history, and the Bible, are polished-
up versions of topics which appeared in *The Hardest Part.*

He starts with another subject that appeared engraved in his
mind: the lie that God wills war. Not for the first time he complains,
"If God wills War, then I am morally mad, and I don't know God
from evil."[31] Then he turns to the lie that man is no more than an
animal. He agrees that like animals people are driven by the need for
food and sex. Unlike animals, they can paint, write poetry, play music,
and relate to the beauty of the world. People can cooperate to invent
machines, build cities, link the world by means of communication.
He sees this as evidence that they are creatures of God and, as such,
they also have the capacity to relate to the God of love.

In a gripping chapter, "The Lie in the Industrial Revolution", he explains that man's abilities brought about industrialization, which was the opportunity for cooperative advance. But employers turned this truth into the lie that industrialization was just about individual gain.

He wrote:

> *Once and for all, let us remember that whatever the rights and wrongs of the present day may be, the burden of shame for its evils must be shouldered by the employers of the nineteenth century, many of whom were as greedy as and as brutally stupid as barn-door fowls… Business became more and more business, which meant that it became more and more inhumane, mechanical and murderous… so they soothed their consciences, and made Christian charity stink in the nostrils of honest men. They gave their goods to feed the poor (the goods they didn't want) and their charity crucified Christ, because it was not true. The very wells of human kindness were poisoned for the world in the days that damned men's souls to build a Church.[32]*

It was not just the bosses. As workers combined in protest so they accepted another lie, namely that only force could win them the fruits of industrialization. He stated, "Labour stands now able to take what it can by force… It has copied the masters and become a big hen."[33] The ensuing class war, he argued, could lead to another Russian revolution, which did not abolish poverty but did install a dictatorship.

Working-class movements wanted to tackle poverty by taking from the rich and giving to the poor. He too wanted to end poverty and wrote, "I believe that hungry children and child waste make God Almighty mad."[34] But, in a chapter entitled "Street Corner Lies", he claimed that it was a lie to think that redistribution would improve matters. He pointed out that only 1,500 people in Britain had an income of over £20,000 a year and if this were to be divided between the population, each person would get an extra four pence. The solution was to increase production and to cooperate to share the proceeds.

Brilliant writer though he was, this is Father Geoffrey at his most inaccurate. He takes the figure of £20,000 as being the average income of the 1,500 rich individuals. He ignores that many of these will have incomes in the millions so that any redistribution would result in far more than four pence per person. Further, he concentrates on incomes while ignoring the wealth held by the rich. In the 1920s, a small minority of the population owned most of the land in Britain, while a larger minority owned factories, coalmines, and much property. The majority in Britain owned no property and received little from investments and shares. Moreover, if production were to be increased by the workers, would owner and directors cooperate in sharing fairly the proceeds? The Labour Party did not think so, and the party as a whole argued for improvement via legislation through a democratically elected parliament. Only a small minority wanted a violent revolution.

Father Geoffrey's suspicious attitude towards organized labour appears in another chapter called "Lies and Equality". He starts by knocking down "the false doctrine that all men are equal".[35] By this he means all men being the same in ability and other attributes and he points out that all people are different, some tall, some short, some musical, some not. In its place, he argues the Christian truth that "all men are of equal worth in the sight of God" and continues, "We recognise that the child of the cobbler has as much right to the best medical treatment as the child of the King."[36]

In fact, his views were similar to those of the Christian socialists he wanted to knock down. The best known was Richard Tawney. In his detailed biography of Tawney, Ross Terrill makes it clear that Tawney did not consider that all people were the same. Rather they were of equal value to God. He explained, "The equal worth of all men is derived from a Christian belief in the fatherhood of God. Men are of equal worth because of their common condition (brotherhood) as sons of God."[37] This brotherhood is a relationship of love which should make them want to share resources and opportunities as equally as possible.

Father Geoffrey and Tawney had similar beliefs. Both asserted that all people were of equal value to God and therefore all had a claim to God's resources. However, they differed on how the end of poverty and other social injustices was to be achieved. Tawney argued that the rich and powerful would never voluntarily agree to share their incomes and wealth more fairly and that therefore the Labour Party had to seek change through politics and trade union activities which complied with the law. Father Geoffrey considered that this meant class warfare and put his faith in all people accepting "The truth that the Secret of Life is service."[38] This could only come about by widespread acceptance of Christianity.

Father Geoffrey's view was that God was the answer. But he didn't mean "The ancient conception of God as an absolute monarch sitting on a throne with a jewelled crown, with the sceptre in His hand."[39] Rather, he believed that it was the God who came as the Christ to serve and suffer. As he put it:

> *That passion in the name of Christ is the only motive which can be made powerful enough to get the world's work done without compulsion, powerful enough to keep us working at our hardest, dealing honestly with our neighbour, denying ourselves the profits of corruption, scheming and lying; powerful enough to ensure the universal rule of Right over Might, and of Justice over Greed.*[40]

This is not the kind of religion that justifies and upholds gross inequalities. He adds, "We do not honour kings as kings. We cannot believe any longer that there can be such a thing as a divine right to rule... the doom of all Kaisers, Czars, snobs, and autocrats is recognised as inevitable and with them must go the old God."[41]

William Purcell does not rate *Lies* highly, saying it lacks cogency, "smacks more of the street corner stand and therefore has less in it of abiding value".[42] On the other hand, Walters writes that it is "an application of the essential principles of Christ... to social and economic problems" and he prints five extracts from it in his anthology.[43] Kenneth Woollcombe said in his lecture, "In the decade after the end of the First World War, he wrote five books. The raciest and, in my opinion, the best of them was *Lies*."[44]

Purcell's comments are understandable. *Lies* is like street corner oratory in its exaggerations, even in its inaccuracies. Yet the hard-hitting street corner style is just what would attract many ordinary readers. As Woollcombe says, it is "the raciest" of his books. Yet it is not facile and he was ready to tackle topics – like challenging the concept of God on a throne and questioning the rights of kings – which other clerics avoided. The test of its popularity was in its sales. The first edition soon sold out and in the next fifteen years was reprinted sixteen times.

### Food for the Fed-Up

*Food for the Fed-Up* appeared early in 1921. On the first page, Father Geoffrey explains that during the war he often heard soldiers complain, "I'm fed-up," which expressed "all the consciousness of waste and futility, all the bitterness of barren agony".[45] After the war, a general unhappiness continued: "There has come upon us a great disillusionment."[46] He had touched upon this subject in talks and previous writings but the whole of the book is devoted to it.

If *Lies* expressed doubts about politics being the answer, *Food for the Fed-Up* comes down heavily on capitalism and free markets with their innate greed. He considers that capitalism in the twentieth century has brought about "a world of selfishness grown more selfish, of greed that has grown more greedy".[47] But greed does not satisfy, and contributes to the emotional depression and unhappiness that grips the nation.

Not surprisingly, he asserts that the answer can be found in Christianity. Unfortunately, he claims, theologians have concentrated on a pessimistic gospel, on subjects like original sin, the fall of man, and eternal punishment. He counters that people need a different gospel, one that uplifts them. He asserts that this can be found in the existing Apostles' Creed – an updated creed which moves with the times.

The book moves through each section of the Creed. He starts with: "Those brave words, I believe in God the Father, Almighty, Maker of Heaven and Earth."[48] He reasons that if God is good then he has made a good earth and given humankind gifts which, if used properly, "enable men to unite, to co-operate, to share a common fund of knowledge of Truth and Beauty. They break down our isolation from one another and draw us into a closer unit. They are a means of increasing Love."[49] But how can the gifts of God be used properly? He turns to the next part of the Creed, which is about Jesus Christ, a saviour "who will not merely change man's lot but can transform man's soul".[50] The power, the love, and the indwelling presence of Christ can enable people to live unselfishly for others.

Next is the part of the Creed which highlights Mary, the mother of Jesus. Father Geoffrey, unlike a small number of liberal clergy of his time, accepts that she was a virgin when Jesus was born and he contrasts her purity with the tide of immorality in the post-war years. Coming up to date, he attacks those who interpreted Sigmund Freud's teachings to promote sexual immorality. They argued that sexual repression led to emotional unhappiness which could be countered by the practice of free love. Father Geoffrey retorts that the reverse is true, that the shedding of marriage promotes family instability, children being separated from parents, and eventual unhappiness for the adults. He concludes that a life based on the examples of Mary and Jesus "leads to clean manhood, clean womanhood and Christian self-respect".[51]

He works through the whole of the Creed which, according to his understanding, is the basis for good relationships with humankind and with God and hence is the source of purpose and joy. His theology emerges as mainly traditional, although dressed in up-to-date language. True, his interpretation that Christ's death at Calvary was not a once-and-for-all event but that rather his suffering continues every time his followers sin and reject him was not mainline Anglican teaching. But he still regarded the cross as central and advocated daily Communion as a celebration of the blood and body given for the forgiveness of his people. He showed that he believed in the incarnation of Christ and the indwelling Holy Spirit.

Father Geoffrey's theology may have been traditional in its acceptance of the basics of the Apostles' Creed. But its application to society was not conservative. From it, he makes the case for an end to "sordid money-grabbing, its cruelty to children… the idiotic trust in forces, building its battle ships and torturing its women, blasted with pride and self-sufficiency".[52] He points to a different kind of society which counters disillusionment and unhappiness.

Purcell wrote that *Food for the Fed-Up* was "the best of Geoffrey's books of this period… a tremendous piece of sustained apologetic".[53] He praised his "ability to go through the Creed clause by clause, re-stating its ancient truths in modern terms, straining every nerve to show its relevance and its necessity; and clothing all in memorable language".[54] He stressed the importance of Father Geoffrey taking on "those arch-enemies of faith – materialism, determinism, pessimism, cynicism – with which he was to be in frequent conflict in print, as on platform and street corner, for the rest of his life".[55]

Walters agreed that it was one of his best books. He noted that, although ostensibly about the Apostles' Creed, "It's actually an attempt to persuade readers that the phenomenon of war need not destroy religious faith. It contains in germ the ideas he would develop over the next decade about the suffering God, evolution, community, Christ, the role of the church, pacifism and the just society."[56]

The street corner style and the rapid, almost machine gun like points in *Lies* are less in evidence in *Food for the Fed-Up*. At times, there are passages of measured beauty, joy, and hope. An example is one of his pieces about the cross:

> *All the sorrows and all the glories of human history surround and are summed up in Calvary. Stand alone on that little hill and you can hear the weeping and the songs of triumph of countless worlds of men and women who have*

*journeyed out of the darkness into the light and out into the darkness again. The heart of humanity turns thither in its bitterest hours, and feels a friend draw near. Explanations seem futile, criticisms become impertinent and absurd. Let it stand alone, that Central Cross, and tell its own heart-piercing tale. Words can only serve to veil its glory and dim the radiance of its beauty for the suffering soul of man.*[57]

## *Democracy and the Dog Collar*

*Democracy and the Dog Collar*, which also appeared in 1921, is the most explicitly political of his books. Father Geoffrey dismisses the opinion that Christians should not get involved in politics and proclaims, "God is the great politician. He is out to build a city – the new Jerusalem – and he has to work through subordinates and trust them."[58] He continues, "with all my heart I believe that the City of God is to be a democracy" so it follows that "We must all be politicians."[59] The book is not an evaluation of which political parties best promote Christian principles. He soon states, "I am not a member of the Labour Party, nor do I propose to become one."[60] Rather it is an examination of the relationship between the church, by which he means organized religion, and the labour movement, which he calls organized labour. Organized religion embraces all denominations. Organized labour stretches beyond the Labour Party and includes trade unions, co-operatives, and other bodies which draw working men together to promote their interests. He gives little attention to organizations of middle- and upper-class people such as owners of capital and members of professions. He asserts that the two great human movements are the church and labour.

The form of the book is a prolonged discussion between two imaginary people. The representative of organized religion, he says, might be a cardinal, a priest or a lay Christian, but it sounds very like Father Geoffrey. The speaker for organized labour, he says, could be a composition of such well-known figures as Mr Hodges, Mr Thomas, Mr Clynes, and Mr Lansbury. He takes it for granted that readers will know who they are. Over eighty years later, it is necessary to explain that Frank Hodges was the moderate secretary of the Miners' Federation, James Henry Thomas was the general secretary of the National Union of Railwaymen, J. R. Clynes was a leading Labour MP who later served in two Labour governments, and George Lansbury – already mentioned in a previous chapter – was the editor of *The Daily Herald*, a strong Christian and Anglican and soon to regain his seat in the Commons.

Each section of the book starts with a short statement likely to come from a person from the Labour movement such as "The worker is concerned with food not faith" and "The Unions are better brotherhoods than the church". The debate then gets under way with Mr Organized Church nearly always getting the last word.

The discussion lacks dynamism and the main value of the book is that it reveals the direction of Father Geoffrey's thinking. In this, he displays a reading of relevant authors such as the economist John Maynard Keynes, the philosopher John Stuart Mill, the Labour writer Sidney Webb, and the Christian socialist MP (and later chancellor of the exchequer) Philip Snowden.

Mr Organized Religion, who will now be called Father Geoffrey, makes the initial point that the church has repented of its overwhelming support of the rich. He points to the Church of England's Lambeth Conference of 1920 where this was much in evidence. Noticeably, although it was previously said that Mr Organized Religion might be a cardinal or from any other denomination, the focus is almost exclusively on the Church of England.

Next Father Geoffrey reveals his ambivalence about social class. He says that he regrets that the church has largely excluded working-class people. He acknowledges that it is wrong that some should live in luxury while others are in poverty. He insists, "We (the church) do not recognise class distinction in any form."[61] Yet soon after he seems to change his stance when he defends class differences. Drawing on the kind of views on eugenics articulated by George Bernard Shaw and H. G. Wells, both of whom he read, he states:

*It is not true that what are called the "upper classes" are only upper through luck, inheritance or fraud. They are upper partly through essential superiority of brain, power and ability... There is no lie more utterly devoid of truth than the lie of the equality of men... There are, and there always will be, enormous inequalities among men in respect of body and brain power.*[62]

Here he is repeating points about equality which he already made in *Lies*. He ends, "I am unequal, and I don't want to abolish the inequality which I believe will always exist."[63]

What is clear is that he does not approve of the labour movement using strikes, which he identifies with class warfare. He concedes that there may be times "when it is absolutely necessary, but when it is it must be recognised as a necessary evil, which must not be allowed to last a moment longer than can possibly be helped".[64] So how can the labour movement achieve improved conditions? He argues that it will succeed by "The essential righteousness of its cause, the appeal which it has made to the conscience of men."[65] A similar pressure has to be applied to those living in luxury: "Surely what we have to do is create a public opinion which condemns and despises idleness and sensuality."[66] In short, change will come from public opinion which makes both the poor and the rich more moral.

He does want an alliance between the church and the labour movement in order to promote a fairer society. However, if this is to happen then the latter must become more Christian. He makes clear:

*Great and powerful as your movement appears to be today, we do not believe that it has any future unless it takes over and adopts as its own the moral and spiritual ideas of Jesus Christ... go for a thoroughly Christian Labour movement; do that and we believe the world is yours.*[67]

He agrees with labour that capitalism is largely evil "because in theory and in practice it was based upon a single incentive, it was based entirely upon one motive of production – the motive of self-interest".[68] Nonetheless, this should not lead to class enmity because, he asserts, some employers did retain the notion of public service and, in cooperation with the labour movement, this could cause capitalism to evolve into a system that served the community.

Of the three main writers about Studdert Kennedy, Grundy and Purcell ignore *Democracy and the Dog Collar*. Walters writes very briefly that it is: "The only one of his books that hasn't aged well."[69]He uses no selection from it in his anthology of Father Geoffrey's writings.

Certainly it is the most disappointing of his books. The idea of a discussion between Mr Organized Church and Mr Organized Labour does not come off. The writing is stilted and long drawn-out. The two men tend to give lectures to each other rather than debate and argue. And, of course, it is not really two men because Father Geoffrey plays both parts. It would have been better if Father Geoffrey and George Lansbury had sat in a pub over pints of beer – well, not for the teetotal Lansbury – and talked, with his reporter friend taking notes. The content is unsatisfactory in that, although Father Geoffrey wants politicians to tackle social injustices, he never explains in detail what he means by this. To what financial extent does he desire the rich to have less and the poor to have more?

He is opposed to trade unions striking to improve their conditions. Instead, he claims that the call for greater morality will somehow bring workers and factory owners together in unity. He does not explain just how this will happen, but he wants the church and the labour movement to be in alliance – providing that the latter turns fully to Christ.

What does become clear is Father Geoffrey's own ambivalent position when he encourages people to be politically active but refuses to join a political party himself. He does not say so but perhaps this is because membership of any party might offend some worshippers. For him, political involvement has two main outlets. The first is to show the extent and effects of poverty through his talks and his writings. His expectation is that he will move politicians to take action and also stimulate a new national morality which will make people more likely to serve each other. The second outlet is the promotion of the church as a national authority on social problems, a voice to which political parties, factory owners, the wealthy, and the workers would listen. Even as these words came into print, he was about to accept a position where his notion of political involvement would be put into practice.

## Leaving St Paul's

On 28 September 1921, *The Worcester Herald* devoted a whole page to a farewell meeting to mark the departure of Father Geoffrey and Emily from the parish. He had become convinced that God was calling him to a wider ministry. The Industrial Christian Fellowship (ICF) was a Christian agency which saw in him the very man to promote their views. It offered him a post as their main speaker and he soon accepted and resigned his position at St Paul's Church.

The meeting was held in the boys' school in order to give space to the large crowd which attended. In the presence of the Dean of Worcester, William Moore Ede, a number of gifts were made to the Studdert Kennedys. The churchwardens presented a silver coffee pot and a cheque. They must have expressed some veiled hostility at the loss of their priest, for the report explained that the dean intervened to point out that "Mr Kennedy was a man with exceptional gifts and that it would be wrong for him to continue to be tied-down to the routine of a parish and not free to exercise his gifts by speaking in various parts of the country".[70]

The altar servers gave him a framed photo of themselves as an expression of their love. Father Geoffrey's own love for the sacrament of Holy Communion must have made it doubly acceptable. Other gifts included an attaché case, a fountain pen, and an ashtray. It was not said at the time but they suited his heavy travelling, writing, and smoking. Emily received a handbag and an early morning tea set.

According to the paper, Father Geoffrey responded with deep emotion and said:

> *Regularity was the very essence of good parish ministry, but with calls to Glasgow one day and Southampton the next it was very difficult to be a reliable person. Postponed duties had been his greatest burden, and they had been a far greater burden to his wife for she had been among them and known what he should and what he would like to have done and was utterly unable to do. A parish should be a perfectly happy family, where the vicar and his wife were not so much leaders as humble brother and sister. Since the war, heaviest was the burden his wife had continually borne for him at home, and for that reason he was more than grateful that they had so completely included her in the presentations.*[71]

Emily responded and

> *...attributed her work to the help of others and the love and gratitude of girls who had always been so very, very willing to assist her... She thanked the members of the working party, who had so often made presentations to her, from the bottom of her heart. Wherever she and her husband went there would never be any place like St Paul's because of its sentimental value. It was their first home after their marriage and their baby was born and christened there. No place would equal it in her mind.*[72]

She then turned to the dean, who "had always been so fatherly towards both her and Mr Kennedy and who 'fathered' her during the war when her husband was away".[73] At this point, the audience burst into applause.

The formal speeches moved the hearers. The Studdert Kennedys were admired throughout the parish. It is appropriate to end with the comment of Arthur Payne, who was there as a boy. He was reported later as saying:

*Even though I was still a boy, I remember vividly the*
*passion of Woodbine Willie's sermons... He never used the*
*pulpit but would sit on the steps of the altar and just talk*
*to everybody. However, he pulled no punches and was very*
*much a working man's priest. He used to hold his St Paul's*
*congregation spellbound.*[74]

The Studdert Kennedys did not leave Worcester. They had to move out of the vicarage but remained in the city in a house in Bromyard Road. He was no longer a parish priest and, for the rest of this book, will be referred to not as Father Geoffrey but as Studdert Kennedy. Money had never worried him and it appears that his salary at the ICF was not high. Moreover, their second son, Christopher, was born on 5 January 1922. The Church of England stepped in to back him in his role as a national preacher. It did so in a practical way by providing some extra income. The Archbishop of Canterbury, Randall Davidson, arranged for him to take over the living of a London church, St Edmund, King and Martyr, in Lombard Street. Previous incumbents had been scholars and students and it was intended that the post would provide him with some money without having to make much input into the church. It did not work out quite like that.

# 9

# THE NATIONAL FIGURE, 1921–29

In the autumn of 1921, Geoffrey Studdert Kennedy was appointed as the messenger – the main speaker – of the ICF and remained in its employ until his death. The ICF still exists, although now as a small charity which describes itself as "an ecumenical organisation to help Christians live out their faith in the work place".[1] On its website, it proudly points back to Studdert Kennedy "as an advocate for the working classes" and quotes one of his radical statements: "If finding God in our churches leads to us losing Him in our factories, then better we tear down those churches, for God must hate the sight of them."[2] It acknowledges that the ICF is not so outspoken today and instead concentrates on helping Christians to practise their faith in the work setting.

## The Industrial Christian Fellowship

So what was the ICF and why did it leap at the opportunity to employ Studdert Kennedy? It arose from the deliberations of one of the committees set up by the National Mission for Repentance and Hope. Its fifth committee, on Christianity and Industrial Problems, argued that cooperation rather than conflict between owners and workers should be a characteristic of industry. Instead of creating an entirely new agency to promote this aim, it drew together two existing bodies. One was the Christian Social Union, which had been established in 1889 and was made up predominantly of Anglicans, especially members of the higher clergy. Its members were often called Christian socialists but this term had two meanings. For some it meant the state promoting greater equality by legislation to redistribute income and power. For others it entailed the pursuit of social righteousness to create a better society. A prominent leader of the Christian Social Union was Henry Scott Holland, a Canon of St Paul's Cathedral and a professor of divinity at Oxford University. He was keen that the Christian Social Union should be more than a talking shop and that members should mix with the victims of poverty. Despite his efforts, by 1919 the number of members had declined sharply.

The other body was the Navvy Mission Society, formed in 1877 by Mrs Elizabeth Garrett to meet the material and spiritual needs of navvies as they moved around building railways, factories, canals, and other large constructions. The society's full-time workers, usually men from working-class backgrounds, and volunteers attempted to evangelize the navvies and encouraged them to avoid alcohol and to work hard. Sometimes they visited and gave material support to their families. These approaches made them acceptable to employers. The number of men required to move around in such building projects dropped, especially as the construction of railways, which had employed many, reached a peak with far fewer jobs on new lines.

These two agencies merged in 1919 to become the ICF. The Reverend P. T. R. Kirk was appointed as director. He had been a vicar in London before serving as a chaplain during the war, where he would have known of Studdert Kennedy. His aims for the new agency were threefold. First, to help the Church of England draw in more working-class people. Second, to enable the owners and managers of industrial concerns to avoid class warfare as they pursued both the good of industry and the well-being of its workers. Third, to campaign for a more socially just society. He regarded it as an advantage that the merging of two different kinds of agencies had brought in both working-class missioners, who were experienced in communicating with ordinary workers, and also well-known clerics who believed that a part of Christianity was a concern for the poor.

## The Composition of the ICF
The direction and tactics of the ICF were much influenced by the 300 members of its council. Details about them have been provided

in a study made by Gerald Studdert-Kennedy, a nephew of Geoffrey Studdert Kennedy. An academic at Birmingham University, his *Dog-Collar Democracy: The Industrial Christian Fellowship 1919– 1929* was published in 1982. This is the only major study of this important but overlooked agency.

The council was made up mainly of Anglicans plus a small number of Nonconformists and even fewer Catholics. New members were appointed by the agreement of existing members. The council then elected an executive of thirty-four.

For the year 1920, Gerald Studdert-Kennedy identified three main groupings among the council members. Most prominent were powerful industrialists, some of whom had close links with the Liberal or Conservative Parties. He gave particular attention to Lionel Hitchens, who emerged as a main leader. Educated at public school and Oxbridge, he rose rapidly to become chairman of the shipbuilders Cammell Laird. During the war, David Lloyd George gave him a number of managerial tasks, which made him well known to leading politicians. He developed a sense of public service and identified with the ICF and its concern for the well-being of employees. Gerald Studdert-Kennedy regarded him as a realist who acknowledged "the bitter antagonism between labour and capital, the extremes of wealth and poverty, the miseries of unemployment, the control that one class has over the lives of others, the greater opportunities of the few and the blank outlook of the many".[3] Hitchens certainly did not favour massive public intervention to change the social order and he regarded inequality as inevitable. But he did want better relationships at work and improved conditions for workers. Gerald Studdert-Kennedy described him and certain other ICF industrial leaders as Christian elitists who believed that industry, inspired by individual Christians, could evolve for the common good.

The next main grouping was a number of Anglican ministers, including several bishops. They included John Kempthorne, Bishop of Lichfield, who chaired the ICF between 1924 and 1937, Charles Gore, Bishop of Oxford, William Temple, who became Bishop of

Manchester in 1921, and George Bell, who was made Bishop of Chichester in 1929. Professor David Thomson, in his history of England of these years, ignored the ICF but did point out that clerics like these "showed that the established church did not irretrievably belong to the Right".[4] Gerald Studdert-Kennedy describes the strong influence Bishop Gore had on Geoffrey Studdert Kennedy. Gore saw poverty as undermining spirituality and stated, "Bad dwellings, inadequate education, inability to use leisure – these are the stones which lie upon the graves of men spiritually dead. We must take away these stones."[5] Geoffrey shared Gore's insistence that the church had a responsibility to tackle poverty. He admired Gore's lifestyle in trying to be close to poor people and refusing the high lifestyle of some bishops. From the written material, there is no evidence of when and how Studdert Kennedy and Gore first met. It may have been at an ICF meeting. Studdert Kennedy did address some of its gatherings in 1920. His interest must have been aroused because by the next year he was a member of its council. Gerald Studdert-Kennedy records that at a council meeting of 12 January 1921, following a discussion of how workers could improve their conditions and wages, Studdert Kennedy "proposed a motion advocating conciliation and arbitration as the only Christian way... and admitting strikes as only a last resort. Gore proposed an amendment recognising the power of the strike in the uplift of workers."[6] No vote was taken and the motion was referred for redrafting. This difference did not stop Studdert Kennedy and Gore cooperating in future ICF activities.

The final grouping identified by Gerald Studdert-Kennedy were labour moderates, often trade union leaders from Nonconformist backgrounds. They were members of the Labour Party but distanced themselves from the militants, particularly members of small revolutionary parties who, in 1920, set up the Communist Party of Great Britain. The militants favoured aggressive tactics such as walkouts, confrontations with managers, and strikes. The moderates considered strikes to be a legitimate tool but were aware that not only did they drain money out of trade union coffers but could also be unpopular with the country as a whole.

Whatever their differences in background and experience, the groups of councillors had a certain unity. The leading industrialists and trade unionists could lobby senior politicians. The Anglican ministers often wrote in religious journals. They contributed to the ICF's own magazine, *The Tablet*, which by 1926 had a circulation of 46,000. Gerald Studdert-Kennedy explained: "The I. C. F.… was the most active and efficiently organised group of Christians seeking to influence the political and industrial climate after the war, and there is ample evidence of the widespread attention it received."[7]

## Political Developments

The ICF appointed Geoffrey Studdert Kennedy as its main missioner partly because of his great abilities as a speaker and writer, particularly in regard to communicating with people of all classes, and also because his views chimed with those of the council members. Like them, he wanted a fairer Britain but not one in which differences in income and wealth completely disappeared. Like them, he favoured moderate not militant tactics. Like them, he believed the church should be more outspoken on political matters.

It is important to put Studdert Kennedy in the context of the politics of the time, for often his public comments sprang from his views on how people were being affected by current policies. Britain remained a nation of great inequality. The historian A. J. P. Taylor wrote: "One per cent of the population owned two thirds of the national wealth; 0.1% owned one third. Three quarters of the population owned less than £100."[8] The Labour Party, committed to a degree of income redistribution, was growing in popularity and won thirteen by-elections between 1918 and 1922 and owned a newspaper, *The Daily Herald,* which was read by many working-class people. Mass unemployment provoked public unrest and the privately owned newspapers voiced fears of a violent revolution. The leader of the coalition government, the Liberal David Lloyd George, had been replaced by the Conservative Andrew Bonar Law. A general election in 1922 gave the Conservatives a clear majority with 347 seats, with Labour's 142 making it the main opposition.

When Bonar Law resigned in May 1923 due to ill health, he was succeeded by Stanley Baldwin, who called a general election on the issue of free trade. Baldwin and his followers favoured making foreign goods more expensive in order to boost British industry and so reduce unemployment. Labour and Liberal MPs countered that it would endanger exports and undermine industry. The outcome was that the Conservatives remained the biggest party but without an overall majority. In January 1924, Labour – with expected support from the Liberals – took power, with Ramsay MacDonald appointed as the first Labour prime minister.

The Labour government was determined to show that it was not extremist despite criticisms from the popular press. It passed some reforming legislation, notably The Housing Act aimed to stimulate council house building. But strikes by dockers and transport workers created divisions between some trade unions and the Labour government. Unemployment was not decreasing and the Labour government resigned in October 1924.

The ensuing election campaign was marked by a letter published in *The Daily Mail* purporting to be from the Russian leadership advising the British Communist Party on how to organize a revolution. It was almost certainly a fake but stoked up fears of Labour, and the Conservatives were returned with a large majority. Stanley Baldwin became prime minister, with Winston Churchill as chancellor of the exchequer and Neville Chamberlain as minister of health. The government improved pensions for widows and elderly people. In regard to the unemployed, it increased the period for which unemployment pay could be claimed but raised contributions and lowered its level. Its major problem was the general strike of 1926. A drop in the demand for coal led to cuts in miners' pay. The government refused calls to maintain their income. When other trade unions backed the miners a general strike started. Within a few days, the TUC (Trades Union Congress), alarmed at the amount of strike pay being distributed and believing that a settlement was near, called off the strike. But the mine owners refused to budge. The miners continued on strike, with their families suffering extreme hardship and by December they had to surrender.

There was a short-lived economic revival in 1928 before 1929 brought in the worldwide economic depression. Such was the political background to Studdert Kennedy's years of national preaching.

## The Crusades

In its efforts both to improve relationships between the owners (and managers) and the workers of industrial concerns and also to draw more working-class people into the church, the ICF ran various activities. Kirk and senior members of the council lobbied MPs and the press. Studdert Kennedy played little part in this. Its working-class missioners still contacted workers in factories, on the shop floor, and in cafés. They met with those out of work in unemployment centres and on street corners. They conveyed the Christian gospel and also helped with material problems. Geoffrey Studdert Kennedy would have felt at home with these grass roots interventions but had little time to take part in them. He did sometimes write for *The Torch* and other journals.

The ICF's major means of proclamation was through its crusades at industrial centres, and he played a major role in these. Crusades meant months of preparation by ICF staff along with local committees of business people and clergy. Once under way, scores of visits were made to churches and factories plus meetings in the open air. Special speakers were brought in including Christian economists, industrialists, trade union leaders, and politicians – George Lansbury was one. Individual conversions to Christianity were welcome but were not the main objective. As the ICF stated, "It is an endeavour to present the Christian religion to the people of a town or district as the solution of the problems of modern social life as they see and experience it."[9] This approach was in keeping with Studdert Kennedy's belief that the acceptance of Christian doctrine and practices would make more people, especially those in industries, more committed to cooperation rather than conflict at work and more ready to promote a socially just society.

Geoffrey Studdert Kennedy was often the star attraction. In 1923, he was in the midst of a great crusade in Stoke-on-Trent and surrounding areas. A curate recorded:

> *Each day the missioners, about eighty of them, met in Hanley Old Church. Bishop Kempthorne of Lichfield was leader but it was Studdert Kennedy who gave the message for the day. In this he excelled. Many people crowded into this meeting just to hear him. Every evening, in one of the Town Halls, there was a mass meeting, often representing some industrial interest. Studdert Kennedy was a necessity here. There was a dinner-hour meeting every day in Stoke Parish Church which held two thousand. It was packed – for Studdert Kennedy.*[10]

The Bishop of Lichfield wrote:

> *He was truly utterly unsparing of himself. He worked from morning till night… His power of sympathy enabled him to appreciate and establish contact with different types of audience – whether it was a mixed meeting in the open air, a drawing room meeting of well-to-do folk, or a congregation of business people at a mid-day service.*[11]

Alan Johnston, in 1925, was an eleven-year-old in Portsmouth where his father was the ICF agent. He recalled hearing Geoffrey Studdert Kennedy speak "at the Guildhall in Portsmouth, packed to the doors with ex-members of the forces, and preached afterwards at our church in Portsea with men sitting on the window-ledges to hear him".[12] When he reached adulthood, Alan trained for the ministry and served as a priest for over thirty years.

A year later, the crusade was in Monmouth, which had strong Nonconformist churches. Their members also flocked to hear him. At the Central Hall in Newport, he condemned the unmitigated harshness of industrial conditions and acknowledged that the church had failed to speak on behalf of the poor. However, he continued that politics was not the answer and said, "Socialism is no use; something more radical has to change the thought of this country. Socialism is rotten, and it is not going to wipe out the slums and poverty you can find any day in Newport."[13] The solution was individuals filled with Christ who would work for the common good.

And so he spoke all over Britain. At Falmouth, with its thriving fishing industry, crowds came to hear him. At Bristol and Croydon, his talks were broadcast. And on to Barrow, Walthamstow, Tyneside, Coventry, Northampton, Mansfield, Battersea, and many other places.

It was not just the crusades. He also spoke at meetings arranged by the ICF which were aimed to reach trade unionists. At least three were made to coincide with the annual conferences of the TUC. At Cardiff in 1921, he addressed 1,200 people. He called for trade union membership to be a basis for fellowship and community. The next year at Stockport, he spoke against strikes and class warfare, and called for their replacement by the practice of mutual service. In 1927, at Edinburgh, he made an attack on trade union agitators.

## Worcester and Elsewhere

As if the ICF meetings were not enough, he still accepted invitations to speak under his own name at other places. He went regularly to the gatherings of the Brotherhood. This now almost forgotten Christian movement originated in West Bromwich in 1875 in order to make the church more acceptable to working-class men. It held Sunday afternoon meetings which were short, lively, and involved some of the men in its running. They also visited and helped neighbours who were in poverty. Sometimes known as Pleasant Sunday Afternoons, it reached a high of 250,000 members in Britain. It did not avoid politics and pressed for and then applauded the introduction of old age pensions. This would have pleased one of its best-known speakers, the one-time Christian socialist leader of the Labour Party, Keir Hardie. Geoffrey Studdert Kennedy welcomed its success in drawing in working people and accepted invitations to address meetings at West Ham, Croydon, Portsmouth, and Southampton, and the Brotherhood's magazine published glowing reviews following his talks. I have a personal interest in that my paternal grandfather was a member of one of the largest branches, which met at the Congregational Church in Ilford.

The fame of Studdert Kennedy prompted numbers of invitations to speak abroad. On at least two occasions, he visited the USA. In 1923, he was accompanied by Emily. He went under the auspices of the Berkeley Divinity School but little is known of his destinations or what he said. However, Purcell did obtain information from a former student who wrote, "I heard him first at the Indianapolis Convention of Student Volunteers in 1923. He electrified the vast audience."[14] In 1924, he travelled – by sea – with Emily, Patrick, Christopher, and a Maud Law who looked after the boys. As mentioned in the previous chapter, he went from the USA to Canada to speak in Toronto. He told a reporter, "I started in the slums. I was eight years in slum parishes at Worcester and Leeds. Our working class is suffering terribly but there is a great change in social conscience. We're beginning to realise how cruelly we took it out of our working class."[15]

The invitations continued to flow in from New York, California, Australia, and South Africa. But Studdert Kennedy called a halt to them in order to concentrate on his work in Britain.

Studdert Kennedy was travelling all over Britain. To get an understanding of his life pattern, it must be appreciated that during this time he spent two days a week with his family in Worcester. While there he spoke at local meetings. It is known that he addressed gatherings at the Royal Infirmary Hospital and the Worcester Wives Fellowship. He always gave the sermon at the Christmas Midnight Mass at St Paul's when the church would be packed out with worshippers standing in the aisles. Nothing is known of what he said at these places. However, the local paper did fully cover a talk he gave to the annual meeting of the Worcester Social Service Union, probably in 1928. The heading in the paper was "Rev.

Studdert Kennedy on the Economic Tragedy". He had dwelt on the plight of the poor and the journalist reported, "He knew what it was like to try and make £3 meet a bill for £6. It kept one awake at night but it was an entirely different matter to wondering whether there would be anything for the next meal."[16] The reporter continued:

> *Describing the destitute condition of a man who had got the sack, Mr Kennedy said he had no other resources but the Labour exchange and the Guardians. The Guardians are the guardians of the poor but they are also guardians of the rates. Sometimes their zeal to protect the rates is greater than their zeal to protect the poor.*[17]

The reporter stated that Studdert Kennedy dismissed Marxist calls for a revolution and then added:

> *What was required was a policy that really roused the whole country to take a part in the decisions made. The working-class people, in his belief, needed to win over to their side men who were not workers in their sense of the word, and who had the sense to sift out these questions and a desire for the welfare of the whole community.*[18]

He went on:

> *Mr Kennedy said that it was not true to say that Christianity was a class thing but it was true that our churches were very much class churches. It was also true that there was a gospel for the one and another gospel for the other. He was not a Socialist or a Bolshevist, and not anything but a common and garden Christian.*[19]

The report ended with the words of Studdert Kennedy, believing "that the separation between Kensington and Bethnal Green should end".[20]

He enjoyed his addresses in Worcester. He enjoyed even more spending time with Emily and his two sons – three after Michael was born in 1927. Studdert Kennedy made sure that they went on holiday together at least two weeks in the year. Never abroad but always at the seaside, particularly at Tenby or Sidmouth. His grandson, Andrew Studdert-Kennedy, recalls that his father Christopher remembered that Studdert Kennedy even "wore his dog collar on the beach".[21] Emily tried to make sure that he took rest and said in a radio interview in 1962:

> *While he was at home, which was generally one or two days a week, he was free from the strain of engagements and activities. For past-times, he enjoyed a game of golf, chess or a concert, and, especially if we had friends in, he loved a musical evening and great discussions. We enjoyed going out to the country on our bicycles and picnics with the children.*[22]

## Achievements of the ICF

Much as he loved being at home with his family, much more of Geoffrey Studdert Kennedy's time was spent with the ICF. How successful was the ICF? It is difficult to assess its achievements, because it was one of a number of agencies and pressure groups trying to shape church and political policies. Kirk wanted it to be a body so respected that government, opposition, and trade unions would welcome its approaches. To an extent this did happen. Gerald Studdert-Kennedy concluded: "It became controversial and well-known, attracting support from politicians in all three parties, from trade unionists and captains of industry, and from the intermediate world of industrial arbitration and social reform."[23]

In 1926, as a general strike approached, the ICF formed a group which succeeded in bringing together representatives of coal owners and trade unionists to meetings held at its London offices. Some trade unionists welcomed their efforts, and Wilkinson points out that the leadership of the ICF believed it had demonstrated "that co-operation rather than competition, arbitration rather than conflict, were to be the guiding principles".[24] But the meetings came to nothing. The general strike took off and ended in bitterness and huge suffering for the families of the striking miners.

The failure of the ICF brought criticisms from a number of sides. Miners' leaders considered it should have been more firmly on their side if it was genuinely in favour of a better deal for the low-paid. Some radical clerics agreed – like the east London priest John Groser, who marched with the strikers. From a different quarter came the criticism of Ralph Inge, Dean of St Paul's Cathedral, and nicknamed "The gloomy dean" because of his right-wing views.[25] He argued that Christians had no right to meddle in politics. The ICF countered that Christians should be concerned with all that happened in God's world and, even if their influence was limited, take some satisfaction in expressing Christian views on political and economic matters.

Geoffrey Studdert Kennedy appears to have refrained from immediate judgements about the general strike. Purcell devotes five pages to the involvement of church leaders and their efforts to end the strike but he makes not one mention of Studdert Kennedy. He did not appear to sit at the tables of arbitration and negotiation. His dislike of strikes was known. Yet, once the general strike had led to great suffering for miners and their families, he gave generously in order to help feed them. In Carlisle in 1926, after declaring that the bishops had been right to intervene in the strike, he did not pronounce on rights and wrongs but preferred to consider other ways of improving the state of industry. He argued that

> *some of the things that would be done would be to eliminate waste, the costs of production would be decreased, lower prices would be aimed at, real wages would be increased so that they could buy more with the wages they would get; the demand would be stimulated and the unemployed would be reabsorbed through the increased demand.*[26]

Whatever his influence on the general strike, any assessment of him in these years should deal with his impact as the chief speaker of the ICF. Gerald Studdert-Kennedy was critical of his uncle's analysis of Britain's problems as presented in his talks. He stated that his arguments were based on "a highly questionable set of assumptions and prejudices about man in relation to society".[27] These assumptions took for granted "a supernatural order, a divine purpose and individual obligations under it".[28] Gerald did not share Geoffrey's religious views. These led Geoffrey to proclaim solutions that were religious in nature and which he believed enabled people to have greater respect for each other and greater desire to serve each other. Instead Gerald gave more attention to an analysis which identified problems as arising from the limitations of capitalism which could be countered by collective social action by people whatever their religious beliefs.

Nonetheless, Gerald Studdert-Kennedy did recognize the effectiveness of his uncle in reaching and influencing large sections of the population. He claims that before him the church had little impact on politics which had become "a virtually secular... debate about economic distribution by Conservatives and the new Labour Party".[29] The ICF changed this and was taken seriously by politicians and the press, and the credit for this, he argued, went to Geoffrey Studdert Kennedy, "who had a national reputation which was enhanced over the last decade of his ministry, as the main speaker, the 'Messenger' for the organisation".[30]

Geoffrey Studdert Kennedy's association with industrialists, his emphasis on cooperation and his criticisms of socialists might lead to the conclusion that he was no radical. Yet journalists often did describe him as such and Gerald Studdert-Kennedy did not dismiss him as a mere conservative. He was a radical but not one who fitted into political parties. He was radical in his fierce denunciation of poverty, in his condemnation of greed and its replacement by lives motivated by service, in his strong desire for peace between social classes, and in his eventual rejection of war. Not least, he was radical in his pleas for the church to shed its domination by the middle classes and for it to be serious in working to bring about a truly Christian society.

## St Edmund's

During these years, Studdert Kennedy was the rector of St Edmund, King and Martyr, in Lombard Street in the City of London. He was there twice a month, usually arriving on a Saturday and leaving on Sunday evening by train for Worcester. Timetables show that he then spent two days at home before leaving for his speaking engagements. A variation was that he was in Worcester on Thursday and Friday before travelling to London on the Saturday.

The church was located amidst offices and shops and was close to the much larger church of St Mary Woolnoth. It did not even possess a rectory. Few people worshipped there, and the church authorities had anticipated that Studdert Kennedy would be able to draw its income without too much input.

He started with some early Sunday morning Communion services after which he invited the communicants to breakfast. They then walked and talked in the small church garden and his interest in them soon developed into friendships. He began to preach, and the quality and dynamism of his words soon drew listeners who often travelled considerable distances to hear him. Another of his gifts came into use. At St Paul's, he had counselled numbers of his working-class parishioners. At St Edmund's, more affluent people queued to speak with him, to bring problems, to seek guidance, to find a caring person. One of the women counselled recalled:

> *The rector would never press confession on anyone... but he would always hear confessions when asked. I went to the rector for my first confession and amongst all the sins I had to confess was one which literally made me squirm to have to mention. He saw how I felt and as I finished he said with infinite tenderness, "Yes, my dear, that's my great temptation too!" Just imagine how that helped me.*[31]

Another woman, who became a regular at St Edmund's, said:

> *I went to that church regularly for the seven years of his ministry there. The service which impressed me most of all was the early 8.30 communion service on the first Sunday in the month when people would come from distances and the service was wonderful, the peace, the colour, the beauty of the little church and the wonderful way in which Studdert Kennedy took it… Some of us would go for a walk and Mr Studdert Kennedy would accompany us before returning to the 11 o'clock service, the sung eucharist, a very beautiful service. Evensong at 6.30, often people waiting in Lombard Street from 4.30 in the afternoon. A very vital point was the beautiful prayers. He would say, "I want you to pray with me tonight" and he would name some people and causes. Then queues to speak to the rector. No-one was ever turned away. He would stay on to help them.*[32]

The advantage of the ministry at St Edmund's was that his ability to deliver services which facilitated deep worship and his Christian concern for individuals were both exercised. The disadvantage was that much of his time was spent sitting on trains.

# 10

# MORE BOOKS, INCLUDING A NOVEL, 1923–29

One consolation of long train journeys was that Studdert Kennedy could continue writing his books. He had the knack of sitting down in a carriage, getting out his pen and notes, shutting the scenery and any other passengers out of his mind, and concentrating on thoughts which he turned into words. In similar fashion, while waiting to speak at meetings, he could close his ears to what was going on around him and put down a few more paragraphs. In these years, he published four more prose books and composed more poems which were absorbed into different versions of his rhymes.

Clearly, the content of these books partly reflects what he was saying in his talks. But it is of interest that three of the books – not *The Word and the Work*, which was very short – contained at least one topic which was barely covered in the talks. These books were *The Wicket Gate* (1923), *I Pronounce Them: A Story of Man and Wife* (1927), and *The Warrior, the Woman and the Christ* (1928). This suggests that in his talks he played down subjects which might not have been acceptable to the ICF but which he could include in books, over which he had full control.

### *The Wicket Gate*

*The Wicket Gate* starts with Studdert Kennedy recalling his mother reading to the family from John Bunyan's *The Pilgrim's Progress*. He draws attention to the dream about the man in rags, which he describes as follows:

> *Then said Evangelist pointing with his finger over a very wide field, Do you see yonder wicket gate? The Man said, No. Then said the other, Do you see yonder shining light? He said,*

*I think I do. Then said Evangelist, Keep that light in your eye,*
*and go up directly thereto: so shalt thou see the gate; at which*
*when thou knockest, it shall be told thee what thou shalt do.*[1]

Studdert Kennedy then explains that, in the present time, people in real rags – the poor and the unemployed – and those in spiritual rags still needed to follow the light to the gate which leads to true religion. In the book, he then opens the gate which leads to the different sections of the Lord's Prayer.

The initial gate is to Our Father, the fatherhood of God. In a moving passage, he recounts how a child loves to be swung in his father's arms and he refers to one of his own sons: "I can see now my own small son standing before me when I have just put him down and saying with shining eyes, 'Do it again, Daddy, do it again.'"[2] He then rejoices that ordinary men and women can be caught up in the arms of their spiritual Father. This is a personal relationship with God and he comments, "There never was so great a need, as there is today, for personal religion – conscious contact of the individual soul with that soul's Saviour."[3]

Working through the Lord's Prayer, the gates open to reveal the fundamentals of Christianity. Christ is the very Son of the Father and he declares, "No man is really born until he is born again and can say, 'I am a son of God.'"[4] He continues through gates which lead to discussions about the role of the church, about death and resurrection. He insists that both death and resurrection are certain and adds, "I am terrified of life without Him for that is Hell."[5]

The initial emphasis is on the individual's personal relationship with God. But Studdert Kennedy is careful to go beyond individuality. Thus all individuals are sons of God, which makes them brothers. It follows that they have responsibilities towards each other; that is, towards a better society. This comes over also in his discussion of the character of God. God is good, a God of peace not war.

Following the war, Studdert Kennedy built up a reputation as an advocate for peace. The Dean of Worcester, William Moore Ede, declared, "He went to the war as to a holy crusade which by victory would vindicate righteousness, but he returned hating the wickedness and folly of war. He became an apostle for peace."[6] In *The Wicket Gate*, more than anywhere else, Studdert Kennedy insists that the church must be for peace and against war. He writes:

> *This is the truth which, becoming concrete in Christ, challenges the world, bidding men see that they can never be saved until they are brave enough to disarm. If the church is brave enough to take up this challenge, she will be brought into inevitable conflict with the world, and her children will be called upon to suffer for their faith. It means that she can have no more to do with Nationalisms and Imperialisms that find their final sanction in force. That she cannot bless national guns and consecrate national colours.*[7]

Studdert Kennedy never spoke in these savage terms about the church's responsibility to back peace and disarmament, whatever the cost, in his talks at ICF meetings. The reason is surely that the ICF's council contained members who would be uneasy, if not outraged, at such statements. Indeed, at one point, its committee turned down a request from him to publish a pamphlet entitled "Christianity and the Right to Lay Down Arms". Gerald Studdert-Kennedy considered that the committee members were frightened of the publicity it might provoke because his previous "anti-war speeches raised questions in the press about his patriotism and integrity".[8] Studdert Kennedy appreciated that his views on peace might divert attention from his other messages for the ICF, so he modified what he said. But he did not keep quiet in his books.

It must be added that he was not an absolute pacifist. He never condemned the British soldiers who fought against Germany in order, as they saw it, to protect their families and country. But he regarded war as an evil which corrupted its participants, deprived families of fathers and sons, and fostered national hatred. He believed that war was against the will of God and called upon all citizens to reject it. Interestingly, his friend Dick Sheppard became the most famous leader of the anti-war movement. But Sheppard did not become an agitator for peace until 1927, while his famous Peace Pledge Union was not formed until 1936.

Studdert Kennedy's strong words did not dent his popularity. *The Wicket Gate* was well received when published in 1923 and was reprinted ten times in the next eleven years.

### *The Word and the Work*

Published in 1925, *The Word and the Work* is Studdert Kennedy's shortest book, just eighty-six pages. In his introduction, the Bishop of London acknowledges that parts are difficult to read but adds, "This book will make people think."[9] It is based on a series of lectures given to a Lenten meditation and is a study of the first fourteen verses of St John's Gospel. It is more academic than his usual books, and the lectures may well have been delivered to a congregation of well-educated Christians.

In the first chapter, he dwells on the words in verse 1: "In the beginning was the Word." Drawing upon the Greek and Hebrew sources of the term "the Word", he reasons that God is eternal, a being with a rational purpose in all that he does, who implants purposes into his human creations. These purposes include a desire to worship and the capacity to look beyond self in order to serve others. In the second chapter, he contrasts these virtues with those atheists who, in his view, see no purpose in life and therefore become consumed with self.

One of the main themes throughout the book is that Christianity cannot be undermined by science. He points out that many early scientists were Christians who argued that the discoveries of science revealed more about the wonders of the universe without threatening belief in God. Turning to other verses in John, he deduces that Christ is unique, that he existed before the world began, that he entered into the world as a helpless baby and now lives both within and outside the world. He concludes that Christ does not contradict the findings of science but provides an understanding which goes beyond them.

Throughout the study, Studdert Kennedy reveals a grasp of intellectual and artistic writers such as the poet Robert Browning, the playwright George Bernard Shaw, and the philosopher Bertrand Russell. He shows that he has been much influenced by the social psychologist William McDougall, who was critical of psychologists and psychiatrists, especially Freudians, who investigated individuals outside of their social context. He acknowledged that group activity could be dangerous – as when a crowd provokes individuals into violent behaviour – but overall he asserted that "only by participating in group life does man become fully man, only so does he rise above the level of the savage".[10] Studdert Kennedy insists that all people need to approach God as individuals but adds, "A solitary Christian is a contradiction in terms."[11] He continues, "Every fresh revival of the New Life was accompanied by some protest against the system which left untouched extremes of wealth and poverty."[12]

*The Word and the Work* was not a popular "hit" like most of his other books. Indeed, it was the only one which was not quickly reprinted. This was hardly surprising given its intellectual tone. But Studdert Kennedy would have been well satisfied if it drew some educated readers into a concern for the well-being of less privileged members of society and into the practice of opening the doors of their churches to all classes.

### *I Pronounce Them: A Story of Man and Wife*

His next book, published in 1927, was dedicated to his family, "Patrick, Christopher, Michael and the mother of the three". *I Pronounce Them: A Story of Man and Wife* was his only novel. Why so after the success of his previous books? He explains in the foreword, "I have written this story because I had to. It would not leave me alone until it was written… I wanted to preach on the meaning of Christian marriage but always I felt that the problems to be faced could not be faced in a sermon."[13]

He might have added that they could not be expressed in his talks for the ICF. In his sermons and talks, he did speak about sexual relationships in general terms, about the rise in divorces, about the needs of illegitimate children, even about the case for free love put by some psychiatrists and writers. But in these addresses, he did not feel he could talk about the individuals he had counselled, those who had sex before marriage, those who wanted out of loveless marriages, those who lived together outside of marriage. He did not feel it appropriate to talk in public about contraception and abortion. In sermons, his views might not be acceptable to the church, his talks not in line with the views of ICF supporters. A novel enabled him to reveal the lives of real people but disguised as fiction and with judgements which were just his own.

The novel is about sexual relationships in the context of Christianity. Two of the main characters are Anglican priests, both of whom have some characteristics drawn from Studdert Kennedy himself. The older one, the Reverend Robert Peterson, had taken holy orders twenty-five years before "not because of any tremendous religious experience but because his father had been a parson before him and he desired to serve his generation, and to stand for what was decent".[14] Peterson had served in slum areas before moving to a poor parish in a cathedral city. During the war, he served as a chaplain and won the Military Cross. Further, although "He had always detested Socialism... there were times now when he could not withhold his sympathy from them even though he thought they were wrong."[15] Clearly Peterson had much in common with Studdert Kennedy. He differed in that his wife had died young, leaving him to bring up his beloved teenage daughter, Robin.

His younger colleague was the Reverend Jim Counihan who, like Studdert Kennedy, was of Irish extraction, smoked heavily, was devoted to his parishioners, loyal to the Church of England, and was a brilliant speaker who was in demand all over the country. In contrast, he had no children and was in an unhappy marriage.

The story revolves around these two clerics, their families, their colleagues, and certain of their parishioners. Jim's beautiful wife had left him for another man by whom she was pregnant. She had wanted a divorce and eventually obtains it. Jim needed love himself but considered that, according to church teaching, a divorcee should not remarry. Two of his parishioners – both of whom he liked and admired – were Maisie, who had separated from a brutal husband by whom she was pregnant, and Charlie, an upright young man who wanted to marry her. Eventually, they move in together, much against the Reverend Jim's advice who considered it sinful. The Reverend Peterson's daughter Robin, a devoted Christian, marries Peter, the son of an elderly, church-going couple. He is handsome, dashing, and talented. Unfortunately, he has a drink problem and sleeps with other women. Robin is torn as to whether, as a Christian, she should remain faithful to him or divorce and remarry. And so on.

The novel is not just about sex and marriage. Studdert Kennedy could not write a book without dwelling on the curse of poverty. Jim moves to lead a mission in a deprived part of London. He has a team of volunteers committed to helping his parishioners. They include Joyce Wetherby and Christian "Gallant" Dayborn – the "Gallant" being a nickname from his heroics in the war during which he lost an arm. She had been educated at an expensive school before the death of a beloved brother at the front moved her to devote the rest of her life to the kind of working-class people about whom he had spoken so warmly. After a course at the London School of Economics, she moved into the mission as a full-time voluntary worker.

When the wealthy blamed the poor for their own poverty, Joyce defended them, saying:

> *I don't believe the so-called better classes are necessarily better stock. The children of the poor would be all right if we could house them properly and give them a decent wage. But it's these weakly mothers worn out with child bearing and the business of disease that makes me mad.*[16]

Joyce and Gallant fall in love. They have a problem about money: not too little but too much. Joyce in particular feels guilty that she has so much while others have so little. Studdert Kennedy comments,

"The utter contrast between the two ends of London, and all that the contrast entailed, had been burned in her soul, and filled her at times with a bitterness and loathing of her own class."[17] As their marriage approached, Joyce and Gallant pondered where to live. One option was a large house in a safe, respectable neighbourhood where they could rest from their exhausting work and provide a better environment for their hoped-for children. But this would distance them from the people they had grown to love and turn them into outsiders who paid patronizing visits to those who had no choice where they lived. They settled on turning a disused factory into a social club for the area with a house attached, where they lived.

Joyce and Gallant married happily. The dilemmas of the other characters had no perfect endings. Maisie and Charlie are never able to marry but remain together. They cannot take Communion but remain followers of Christ. The Reverend Jim has to question the rigidity of the church's teaching and he remains their friend. When Maisie and Charlie have a baby girl, he gladly agrees to baptize her. Jim and Robin fall in love. Both are divorced by this time and legally allowed to wed. Yet both feel that to do so is against Christian law. The book ends with them heartbroken and the words, "Behind them both I see the figure of Jesus of Nazareth standing, but his back is turned to me, and I cannot see His face."[18]

William Temple – a well-read bishop if ever there was one – writes of this ending:

> *There is no stronger or more persuasive statement of the Christian law of marriage, with the demand for bitter sacrifice which it may entail, than the closing chapters… nor any more searching challenge to faith than the vision of Christ's appearing behind the lovers who, for His sake, part from one another.*[19]

His words seem to congratulate Jim and Robin on their decision not to marry. I do not think this is what Studdert Kennedy is saying. He is a strong upholder of the sanctity of marriage but here he appears to question the church's teaching on the marriage of divorcees. His book is a detailed examination of the complexities and agonies of Christian lovers.

Purcell dismisses the book with the comment, "Clearly the writing of novels was not his line."[20] I disagree. It is an important book. Its main theme is how to bring together the love which Jesus Christ displayed towards people, like the woman taken in adultery, with the laws of a church which rightly wants to uphold sexual morality. Its spin-off theme is about how affluent people, who side with the poor, should refuse to be distanced from them. These issues are still debated and make the book worth reading today. Certainly, the reading public of the time seized upon it. Published in March 1927, it sold out almost immediately and was reprinted in the same month and in April. It was also successfully adapted for the stage at the Everyman Theatre, which is well known as a centre for innovative plays.

### The Warrior, the Woman and the Christ

The subject of sex reappeared in his next book. This is not a novel about individuals but an examination of how the patterns of sexual behaviour have shaped society. He goes back to the early times before marriage was known. Men – he names them warriors – were hunters who slew animals to obtain food. They used women, who were physically weaker, for sexual enjoyment, and to look after children. Women became childminders and homeworkers, dependent on men for food and protection. These unequal power divisions continued throughout history. In the nineteenth century, they were incorporated into capitalism, which became a field "where the warrior displayed his prowess and went to war. The pursuit of wealth becomes an end in itself as the hunt and the battle had done in former days."[21]

There follows Studdert Kennedy's most strident criticisms of capitalism, much stronger than in his talks for the ICF. He states that capitalism treated working-class children and women as economic units who toiled long hours in industry for meagre wages.

Working-class men were also exploited, so deepening the economic and social divisions within Britain. The warrior capitalists argued falsely that "cut-throat competition would inevitably and by iron economic law issue in prosperity for all".[22] Middle-class Victorian women were also kept in subjection as wives who organized the home and the children, attended church, and had few rights in regard to property ownership and none at all in regard to having the vote. The warriors were also left free to enjoy sexual behaviour barred to their wives. Numbers consorted with prostitutes who were eventually cast aside to spend their remaining days in poverty and shame. In short, the pattern of sexual relationships had shaped – or misshaped – both industrial and domestic life to the overwhelming advantage of the warriors.

Studdert Kennedy perceives the start of improvements in the Victorian years thanks to religion. A number of Christian leaders spoke out against the hardships caused by capitalism. These included the Conservative, Lord Salisbury, and the early Christian socialists, Canon Charles Kingsley and the Reverend Frederick Maurice. They argued that the economic and social developments were contrary to the teachings of Christ. A smaller number of Christian women were also influential. Most notable was Josephine Butler, who campaigned for higher education for women and also strove to improve the lot of prostitutes.

By the twentieth century, Studdert Kennedy saw signs that men were becoming less warrior-like and women more participative in decisions regarding home life. He concluded, "We have Christ's authority for believing that the full significance of the sex relationship can only be realised when two free, equal, consecrated personalities enter into a voluntary, life-long, indissoluble union of mutual love and service to God, to one another and to their children."[23] This building of good homes benefits not just the immediate family. He goes on, "A home is a little world, a miniature society, and in it the great social problems present themselves for solutions."[24] Thus, according to Studdert Kennedy, the Christian family, where husbands and wives are sexual equals with both involved in child care, is the basis of the good society, indeed of world peace. However, it is less clear just how this happens, how family relationships are transferred to the wider sphere. As Purcell commented on this book, "The impression is of someone attempting to cover so wide a ground of speculation that sight is lost of the original point of departure."[25]

The clearest and most inspiring part of the book is his final deduction that Christ is God's Son and is also a mixture of warrior and woman. He was a warrior in his conflict with Jewish and Roman authorities, in his refusal to give in to Satan's temptations, in his courage on the cross. He was woman in his gentleness, his compassion, his love of children, and his servanthood. Studdert Kennedy concludes, "It is in this perfect unity in Him that I find the keystone to the quality of His Life. He was the man woman, the mother father, the creative warrior complete."[26] He is the model for both men and women, and both sexes should be drawn to worship him and together contribute to the transformation of society.

Studdert Kennedy's thesis is that the physical strength of early men set a pattern of male domination and female subjection which formed a society of sexual inequality that was later expressed in the inequalities of capitalism. This is just stated not proved. Whether it is historically sound or not, this conviction does lead to some of his most radical writing. His criticism of capitalism and its advocates is almost bitter. His criticism of socialism is less so and he acknowledges that state education has an important part to play in reducing inequalities. Even more radical for a 1920s Church of England cleric, he recognizes that women should play a fuller role in society. Theologically, his concept of the Christ as a mixture of male and female is years before its time.

Published in September 1928, the book was soon reprinted in January and September 1929. It must have gone on selling, for a letter reached his wife Emily in March 1939 from a rector in a church in Vermont, USA. He wrote:

*As each Lent comes round I re-read your husband's books. This year I have read* The Warrior, the Woman and the Christ *and am reading* The Hardest Part *to my girls at the school here. They are all thrilled and the books have been a tremendous help. The books compel thought so consistently. I owe much to the fact that your husband's books have taught me to think. They have also been a source of comfort in sorrow. I lost two children by drowning in 1935.*[27]

## The Height of His Popularity – and the End

During 1928–29, Studdert Kennedy was being invited to address large meetings all over Britain. His books were sell-outs with numerous reprintings. He received coverage in both the religious and national press. In 1928, *The Radio Times* invited him to contribute. Established in 1923, it had quickly risen to being the magazine with the highest circulation in Europe, with articles written by leading media, literary, and political figures. In introducing his piece, the magazine stated, "Few preachers and writers have so wide and eager a public as 'Woodbine Willie'. The reputation which he gained during the war from the fearless simplicity of his philosophy clings to him still in peace. This article is, therefore, a notable feature of our Spring number."[28] In an article entitled "Whither? And Why?", he wrote a straightforward repudiation of atheism and agnosticism followed by a proclamation of Christianity.

In 1929, he was asked to do a series in the popular *The Pictorial Weekly*. His first piece appeared in April, where he introduced his subject as Jesus' Sermon on the Mount and its relevance to modern living. He was at the height of his fame. But by that time he was dead.

# 11

# THE DEATH OF STUDDERT KENNEDY, 1929

### "I Have No Strength for More"

In March 1929, Britain was hit by a flu epidemic. Geoffrey Studdert Kennedy had been feeling ill, he was very tired, and his asthma was troubling him. But he was committed to returning to Liverpool to do a series of Lenten lectures at Liverpool Parish Church where an old friend, the Reverend Edward Harrison, was vicar and all the preparation and publicity was in place. He hated letting people down and decided he had to go. At the gate of his house in Bromyard Road, he hesitated and then went back inside. Emily and the three boys were also unwell. He climbed the stairs and his wife assured him that she could cope. He left and made the familiar walk to the railway station. He was never to see his family again.

Soon after arriving at St Catherine's vicarage in Liverpool, his symptoms worsened. He took to bed and it became apparent that he had pneumonia. Emily was summoned and their good friend, William Moore Ede, drove her to Liverpool. On her arrival, her husband was unconscious and soon after died at 1.30 a.m. on 8 March 1929 at the age of forty-five.

He had died of pneumonia, no doubt made worse by his asthma and smoking. In addition, he had been following an exhausting work programme which must have hindered his efforts to combat serious illness. His engagement diary shows that between 21 November 1928 and 7 March 1929 he spoke at 37 places in 107 days throughout England, Wales, Scotland, and Northern Ireland. He usually gave several talks at each destination, so they would have numbered over a hundred. In between, he was on trains, preparing his talks and writing for publication. Noticeably, he had been addressing meetings in Liverpool before dashing home to see his family and then returning to undertake the Lenten lectures. A report in the *Liverpool Echo* perceptively observed:

> *We feel that this tragedy lies at our door. It is a curious fact that though Liverpool can arrange more successful meetings than any provincial town, except Manchester, it is very difficult to get first class speakers to visit us. As a result, when we do get them we work them for all they are worth… He [Studdert Kennedy] was obviously ill and over-worked, but with quenchless enthusiasm, which seemed to burn through his being, he would not give in. Then he had to take to his bed; a serious change manifested itself and he passed away.[1]*

In a sermon at St Mary's, Oxford, which was reported in the local press, the Reverend Frank Barry, who had known him for twenty years, stated, "When God raises up a prophet for us we do not stone him or persecute him: we either ignore him or kill him with overwork."[2]

Much as he was pressed by others to overwork, it must be added that Studdert Kennedy did not require much persuasion. Prebendary Linsley was beside him during much of an ICF crusade and recorded, "Giving of himself to the uttermost, 110 per cent, and coming back to our vicarage flattened him out. He'd given all. It was rather distressing to see the cost of giving."[3] The Reverend Dick Sheppard also saw much of him and wrote:

> *When I last saw him, I told him he could not go on for long at the pace he was working, making lightening journeys north, south, east and west, to deliver half a dozen sermons or speeches at each destination, with never a moment's thought for himself; but he laughed my fears away. He persuaded me that he was the one exception who could tour the country unceasingly, and yet retain his freshness, vigour and health. But it was not to be. He died at the height of his power through reckless attention to duty and refusal to give in though he was gripped with illness and pain.[4]*

Andrew Studdert-Kennedy – whose father Christopher was seven when Geoffrey Studdert Kennedy died – has thought much about his death and commented that his grandfather was compelled by the Spirit of God "yet there is something absolutely relentless about it and he was driven into the wilderness".[5]

Perhaps Studdert Kennedy felt both compelled and worn out and was ready for eternal rest. His poem entitled "It is Not Finished" ends with the lines:

> *The stars are coming out,*
> *My body needs its bed.*
> *I have no strength for more,*
> *So it must stand or fall – Dear Lord –*
> *That's all.*

## The Funeral of "A National Figure"

Studdert Kennedy's body was removed from the vicarage to lie at St Catherine's Church. News of his death spread quickly, and over 2,000 people filed past his coffin to pay their homage. Grundy writes: "Immediately there was a proposal that he be buried in Westminster Abbey but the Dean of the day is reported as having exclaimed, 'What! Studdert Kennedy! He was a socialist.'"[6] Just as well, for he would have wanted to be buried in his beloved Worcester. And by Sunday he had been transported there.

When the coffin was unloaded at Worcester, the streets were full of mourners as his body was taken to St Paul's Church where a short service was held for family and friends. On Monday, the church was open and a parishioner recalled, "I was one of the four chosen to stand at his coffin in St Paul's on the day before the funeral. People filed past in their hundreds – needless to say they came from all walks of life."[7] Many workers from the nearby factories came in their lunch hour. Two services of Holy Communion were held, one taken by his brother, the Reverend William Studdert Kennedy, assisted by his lifelong friend, the Reverend J. K. Mozley, which Emily attended.

The funeral was held on Tuesday 12 March. The cortege drove slowly to the cathedral. In the parish of St Paul's every home had its blinds drawn. Parishioners had contributed – mainly in pennies – to a huge wreath carried on the coffin. At it passed St John's School, the pupils lined the school railings in silence. In the city, shops had lowered black shutters. The streets were crowded with mourners and over a hundred unemployed men marched from the labour exchange to the cathedral, with their leader carrying a cross of tulips. Over 2,000 waited inside the cathedral, headed by Emily, their eleven-year-old son Patrick, and Studdert Kennedy's brother, the Reverend William Studdert Kennedy. The Reverend P. T. R. Kirk represented the ICF. Afterwards, at St John's Cemetery, ex-servicemen threw packets of Woodbines onto the coffin. But Emily was not there. On the drive she had felt too overcome and returned to her home at Bromyard Road.

On the same day, memorial services were held at other places, including St Martin-in-the-Fields where his brother Maurice was among the nearly 3,000 attendees. There was also one at St Ann's in Manchester where Studdert Kennedy had been scheduled to talk that very day. The church was so full that many knelt in the aisles. At Liverpool Parish Church, the Reverend A. Shields, northern director of the ICF, remembered Studdert Kennedy taking off his boots and giving them to a needy man in the street. Another service was conducted at Risca in a deprived part of South Wales where he had become popular. The local scout troop, known as Woodbine Willie's Own, were on parade. He would have liked that.

The huge crowds at Liverpool and Worcester and the almost impromptu services at places where he had preached led the thoughtful William Purcell to write, "One thing became immediately apparent. Geoffrey had been a national figure to a degree which would probably have astonished him more than anyone else."[8] He adds that he was a national figure with a difference. Whereas most people in this category, like politicians and royalty, were both wealthy and distant from ordinary people, Studdert Kennedy was at one with them both financially and socially.

Indeed, the state of his finances meant that he had not left his family in economic comfort. His salary had never been high, although the income from his books was substantial. However, he gave most of it away, particularly to charities. Purcell records that, at St Edmunds, he was given a cheque for £200 as an Easter gift but "he had given it immediately, somewhat to the indignation of the donors, to the Miners' Distress Fund then in operation".[9] He had made out a will on the torn out page of a notebook, leaving the house and about £150 a year to Emily. It was hardly sufficient for a family of four. His admirers rallied around and a letter was sent to the church press from Randall Davidson, Archbishop of Canterbury, and his clerical friends William Moore Ede, P. T. R. Kirk, J. K. Mozley, Dick Sheppard, and William Temple. It explained that

> *his sudden death had left his wife and three boys with totally inadequate provision for the future... His love for the needy and all in distress made him indiscriminating in his gifts; he gave away every penny of his income, apart from what was necessary for the support of his family and for his own simple needs. For many years he was very poor, though in the last few years he earned a fair income, his generous impulses made it difficult for him to save; his thoughts were always for others, never for himself.*[10]

An appeal for funds was made, to which *The Sunday Pictorial* also gave publicity. One of the first to respond was King George V, who sent £100. In all, over £7,000 was raised, which allowed an annual income of £500. In addition, other private donors contributed to fees for the education of the boys.

Studdert Kennedy's national standing was also expressed in the coverage in the national and provincial newspapers. Grundy wrote, "News of his death was deeply felt across the nation and reflected in glowing obituaries in the press from *The Times* to the *Morning Star*"[11] (that is, from a Conservative paper to a Communist one).

*The Daily Telegraph* hailed him as a great popular preacher and said:

*With an attractive easy manner, a great sense of humour, and a remarkable command of the direct and telling speech of the man in the street, he attacked social evils fearlessly. Rich and poor alike flocked to his church. His preaching was eloquent, passionate and sometimes incoherent, but it never failed to hold hearers fascinated. The unhappy and the disinherited, the failures of this world and the buffeted seldom had a more heartening and valiant champion than Studdert Kennedy.*[12]

*The Morning Post* pointed out that he developed his ability to talk to working-class men when he was a chaplain. It stated:

*As a padre he used to speak to the soldier in a direct, manly way with an instant and enduring appeal. The helpful advice he subsequently gave to all who asked him gained him immense influence with ex-Service men of all ranks... His war experiences had filled him with a hatred of militarism, and his sermons often had as their theme the need for peace... The Rev. P. B. Clayton, the founder of Toc H, wrote of him yesterday that he had carried the good news of salvation to more men of our race than any other living minister in Christendom.*[13]

*The Sunday Chronicle*'s regular columnist, who wrote under the pen name of Mayfairy, recalled how he met Studdert Kennedy during the war. He explained:

*We had just come out of the line. I was tired, hungry and dispirited and felt in no mood for a conventional parson in the field, however good he might have been. He introduced himself as Woodbine Willie and after a few minutes' conversation I could believe all that I had heard about him. The men used to say that there was hardly any at the front would not do any mortal thing for him. Not long after our first meeting, I saw him accompanying the troops into battle, armed only with packets of cigarettes for the wounded. "I am going over the top with you, boys," he had intimated the previous night. To which we all suggested that he should not. He replied that he dare not ask the men to face what he would not, and he knew they would like to be beside him... Studdert Kennedy was particularly proud of the fact that he did not carry what he called his "little parochial religion" and his "silly little parochial God" to the front. And it was undoubtedly this curiously outspoken Christian teaching in the field, coupled with his deep humanity and unfailing joviality, which won him such popularity. This was the padre whom, indeed, Thomas Atkins swore by, whose very name breathed loving tenderness or good fellowship, who used to do thousands of little services for the men.*[14]

*The Liverpool Echo*, in a piece two days after reporting his death, discussed why he was so well known. It wrote:

*What were the secrets of his popularity? It was not that he was a great theologian. In fact, with playful exaggeration, he often declared himself to be ignorant of theology. And in this month's* Liverpool Review *a writer describes the framework on which he sets out his convictions as "inadequate", "almost absurd" and "pure patripassionism" and that "he has not fashioned his knowledge into a system that will bear examination." Again Studdert Kennedy had not the presence, voice, or message of the orator. Neither was it his sensationalism, his freedom and frankness of speech – more characteristic of the trenches than of the sanctuary. Thus the fact that Studdert Kennedy came year after year and packed St Nicholas Church and our largest halls, compelled even those who criticized his methods to admit that he was a man with a message. That was just it! A man of intense vitality, glowing with compassionate sympathy, tortured by pity*

*for human suffering and feeling that he had a message for*
*mankind, he gave himself with it, with an utterly reckless*
*and unselfish generosity. May he rest in peace.*[15]

*The Worcestershire Echo* of 11 March 1929 contained a piece by the Dean of Worcester, William Moore Ede. It was published on the day before the funeral and much of it was spoken by him on that occasion. His themes were to outline the many abilities possessed by Studdert Kennedy and to declare that his message was conveyed worldwide. His article included the following:

> *He gave health and strength with all his remarkable powers of*
> *mind and speech to bring men everywhere to see in the Cross the*
> *solution of the world, and it is by the way of the Cross and by*
> *that way alone the nations of the world can be saved... From*
> *a crusade against war between nations, he turned to devote*
> *his life to a crusade against economic war. He preached peace*
> *at home and proclaimed that the solution between conflicts*
> *between capital and labour, between class and class, was to be*
> *found in the teaching of Christ carried into international and*
> *industrial life. He became an ardent apostle of peace and often*
> *here, in Worcester, dwelt on the wickedness and folly of war. He*
> *did so last Armistice Day, when preaching in this pulpit.*[16]

Numbers of other newspapers carried his praise. The reaction to his passing did indeed reveal that Studdert Kennedy was a popular and national figure in the 1920s. Yet he did not seem to see himself as that. As the Dean of Worcester put it, "The man who was in such demand, who was sure of an audience wherever he went, might naturally have got puffed up, but he was the most humble-minded of men. He never put on side."[17]

## Clerical Obituaries

Studdert Kennedy was also well known among other Church of England clerics. They were less interested in his national fame and more in his theological views and his contribution to the advancement of Christianity. A number wrote obituaries, usually in the religious press, and they contain themes that recur. First, the words "love" and "loved" often appear. Soon after his death, a window was installed and dedicated to his memory at St Paul's Church, which can still be seen there. Emily and her sons were present at the dedication service conducted by the now Canon J. K. Mozley. He said that the window was a remembrance of "the beauty of being well-loved".[18] Referring back to the funeral, he went on, "The reverence with which the streets of the city were full, the multitudes who came together to pay their tribute on that day were moved by a feeling which could not be explained by another word except that of love."[19]

The Reverend Edward Harrison, who had frequently invited Studdert Kennedy to Liverpool and in whose home he died, wrote in a Liverpool magazine that "all the time he was aglow with the love of the Divine Christ".[20] Studdert Kennedy was loved and he loved.

Second, his colleagues spoke highly of his ability to convey the gospel. The Reverend Pat McCormick, who had sometimes stayed with Geoffrey and Emily in their home, wrote in *The St Martin's Review* of how he had profited from his preaching: "I own to having sat at his feet and learned truths from him which have made all the difference to my life and faith."[21] The Reverend Frank Barry, a former chaplain and, by this time, the vicar of St Mary's in Oxford, wrote about his wider impact:

> *He, with Tubby Clayton and Dick Sheppard, are probably the only parsons of whom the man in the street had ever heard of and for whose opinion he much cares. There is none in our whole ministry who had a further reaching influence – or who has done more for the evangelization of English people both at home and throughout the world. His name would pack any building in England.*[22]

Dick Sheppard, also writing in *The St Martin's Review*, stated:

*I have never heard speaking or preaching more sincere, more intelligent, and yet more human. His voice counted, I believe, as much as any in England today... Those who went to hear him would never have come away merely saying, "What an orator." They would have been impressed with his power of speech but, above all, they would have been conscious of having heard a voice that spoke to their very souls and said, "Thou art the man."* [23]

William Temple added, in a book put together quickly by his friends, that it should not be thought that Studdert Kennedy was a facile speaker who relied upon eloquence alone.

*He was far more of a student than either his admirers or his critics were usually aware... He was never content to go to the writers who pass on the thoughts of others; he went direct to the great thinkers. So he travelled over England proclaiming the sacred cause of social justice with a mind increasingly stored with the fruits of economic and social study.* [24]

Third, not surprisingly, the clerics identified the key factors in his theology. Temple, himself a prolific writer and theologian, highlighted Studdert Kennedy's ability to hold the three persons of the Trinity as a unity. He explained:

*To most Christians one of the Persons [of the Trinity] is less in the primary focus of attention than the others but to him the Three Persons were equally real: the worship of his whole being was equally given to each... God is all the Beauty and all the Love that there is; but He is also more than this; and is not only the actual Love and Beauty in the world but is the living personal Spirit of Love and Beauty, by whose presence and energy mountains and flowers are beautiful or men are loving. And all of this found its perfect expression in the life of Jesus Christ.* [25]

Without disagreeing with Temple, the Reverend Frank Barry asserted: "The Cross was the centre of his whole life and outlook – at times he was almost blinded with the light of it… and God was within it, redeeming by his suffering – 'ever crucified and ever rising again'. Studdert Kennedy ventures as far as a man can go in his insistence on a suffering God." Barry adds that the cross is the means of spiritual salvation but not just that. "Behind the Cross there is a sepulchre and the sepulchre is empty. And he preached this for the I. C. F. as the only hope of social regeneration and the Christianisation of economic life."[26]

His friend and colleague, the Reverend P. T. R. Kirk, in a long tribute in *The Church of England Newspaper*, agreed that Studdert Kennedy was a theologian but added that his theology was more than academic theory, it was practical and personal. He wrote:

> *Studdert Kennedy did not care much about theological subtleties. You might think that he had forgotten all that he ever learned about them. It was only with subtleties that he had dispensed; he had a profound and consistent theology, and was most convincing on the doctrines on which most theologians go to pieces. After all, a doctrine is only valuable as it has a practical side. If there were no practical side to any idea that was presented to him by the schools, he had no use for it. But a doctrine can only be understood from the inside – as it is the expression of an experience. That is why so many books on the Atonement of Christ are passed by as being merely words. When Kennedy spoke about the Death of Jesus, it was no formal dogma he offered. He knew what it meant apart from reasoning, for he had been into the depths of human sin and shame as his Master had, and had shared in the same redemptive suffering.*[27]

William Temple agreed that his theology was practical. Its application was revealed in his priesthood. He explained, "If to be a priest is to carry others on the heart and offer them with self in the sacrifice of human nature – the Body and the Blood – to God the Father of our Lord Jesus Christ, then Geoffrey Studdert Kennedy was the finest priest that I have known."[28]

Fourth, it was the theologians who tended to make reference to his opposition to war and his pleas for peace. The Dean of Worcester, William Moore Ede, did so when he spoke at the funeral service. So did the Reverend Edward Harrison who, after pointing to his exploits as a wartime chaplain, wrote: "In the succeeding decades he became no less surely then the apostle of peace."[29] He added, "And it was a great thing to have a Military Cross holder, whose patriotism was unquestionable, and who had been over and over again in the heat of battle, denounce war and the mind that can lead to war."[30]

Studdert Kennedy's clerical friends, in their response to his death, portrayed him as a man of love, as a superb communicator, as having a distinctive, thought-out, and practical theology, and as being an advocate of peace. The Reverend Dick Sheppard shared platforms with him to oppose war. But his final summing up went even wider:

> *I do not write extravagantly if I say that there is no man to fill Studdert Kennedy's place, and that such a combination of gifts as he possessed does not belong, as far as I know, to any living man... It is not in Mayfair, or indeed in Church circles, that his loss will be chiefly felt, but wherever men and women with courage and hope are facing the problems of today meet together.*[31]

## Letters

Amidst all the public tributes to Studdert Kennedy, it could be forgotten that the persons most bereft by his death were Emily and the three boys. Of course, she would have been relieved that his former colleagues ensured adequate financial income for the family. In addition, she received over 300 personal letters of condolence. A telegram from Lord Stamfordham stated, "I am desired to assure you of the heartfelt sympathy of the King and Queen in your great sorrow in the death of your husband. The King has lost a valued chaplain and one who frequently preached at Buckingham Palace.

His work in war and peace will be gratefully remembered."[32]

Many clergy sent personal letters. The Archbishop of Canterbury, Cosmo Lang, wrote, "He was in many ways unique. God gave him a real prophetic gift."[33] The former archbishop, Randall Davidson, penned, "All England mourns with you today... To few men of our age has it been granted to secure the attention of so great a multitude of his contemporaries as he pleaded the cause of God and made sacred things glow afresh."[34] The Dean of Canterbury, George Bell, who was much in sympathy with Studdert Kennedy's advocacy of peace, said, "Your husband was a wonderful man. A real prophet and inspiration."[35] William Temple included in his letter the words, "And he became one of my best friends. So we know something of what it means to you."[36] His wife Frances added in a separate, handwritten letter, "To both of us your husband has always been such an inspiration and such a dear friend... will you later on spare us some of the friendship we valued so much from him and come to see us here?"[37] Dick Sheppard wrote movingly, "I just can't get you and Studdert and the little family out of my mind. None of us can hope to see his likeness again."[38]

Letters were also received from many people Emily had never met. They included ex-soldiers of whom just one example can be given. A former lieutenant recalled:

> He was with my battalion during the war when I soon learned to respect him for his manliness, his courage and his broad-minded Christianity. He earned the genuine affection of every one of us. In September, 1918 during our attack on the Hindenburgh Line, he was gassed the night before we went over the top, but thirty six hours later, when he dropped, he had been helping the doctor with the wounded without a rest. One of God's good men and a type of parson all too scarce.[39]

Other letters came from priests. One described himself as "a young clergyman who owes to your husband all the inspiration and vision which brought him into the ministry".[40]

Not least was a letter which read, "I am just an ordinary working girl but have always made time to go and have my soul filled with just a few of the wonderful inspiring messages that Mr Kennedy gave us. There has only lived one Woodbine Willie just as there only lived one Jesus Christ. He was the most Christ-like man that ever lived. His works will live forever."[41]

Other people contributed to memorials. Studdert Kennedy was born in Quarry Bank, Leeds, where he attended, was confirmed at, and sang in the choir of St Mary's Church. Later he served as a curate there with his father. Soon after his death, an oak lectern was placed at the front in memory of him. At Worcester Cathedral, a bronze tablet was unveiled by the dean and is still pointed out in guided tours. Its words stand out:

> *Geoffrey Anketell Studdert Kennedy MC. A Poet: A Prophet: A Passionate Seeker After Truth: An Ardent Advocate Of Christian Fellowship: Chaplain To H.M. King George V: Chaplain To The Forces: Rector of S. Edmund King And Martyr In The City Of London: Sometime Vicar Of S. Pauls In This City. Born 27 June 1883. Died 8 March 1929.*

## His Last Book

Following Studdert Kennedy's death, the Reverend Arthur Hird, an employee of his publisher, Hodder & Stoughton, came across some of his notes for addresses to retreats and for talks he was preparing with a view to publication. He started to put them into shape for a last book but, unfortunately, died suddenly. William Moore Ede, the Dean of Worcester, took on the task and gave the book the title of its first chapter, *The New Man in Christ*.

In a preface, Moore Ede points out that the retreats usually consisted of small numbers of educated believers, so his addresses and the chapters based on them were somewhat more formal in character than most of his previous books. He adds that, as the editor, he had to cope with parts which were very abbreviated and, in some cases, he just left the headings to stand alone. The last third of the book consists of what appear to be intended for publication as articles and so are more in his usual style. The book was not published until March 1932, when it immediately sold out and was reprinted within weeks.

The first chapter is on a favourite Studdert Kennedy theme, the new life in Christ. He points out that conversion to Christ "may come suddenly but normally it comes gradually".[42] Thereafter individual Christians grow stronger as they go through the experiences of temptation, transfiguration, Gethsemane, Calvary, the ascension, and Whitsuntide. He dwells on Whitsuntide with its stress on the Holy Spirit and he urges Christians to accept the gifts of the Spirit. He draws attention to "the gift of healing which has been lost sight of for so long".[43]

Among the gifts are those of lowliness and meekness. Lowliness is humility towards God, "a deep-seated conviction that the world belongs to God".[44] Meekness "is our attitude towards people".[45] He insists that the church needs people who are filled with the Holy Spirit.

The many tributes paid to Studdert Kennedy following his death depict him as a famous war hero, the church's best-known preacher who filled halls to capacity, a national figure. But there was another Studdert Kennedy as revealed in his last book. It was the priest who loved to withdraw to be in small retreats where he could enjoy fellowship, study, and worship with a handful of Christians. Perhaps it was here that he asked God for the lowliness and meekness which others noticed in him.

In the last paragraph he ever wrote for publication, he ends on an optimistic note. He declares:

> *This new age is a challenge and a call to which we can and will respond as we become filled with the Spirit of Him who made a home at Nazareth and was crowned King of Kings with a crown of thorns and stoned on Calvary. The courage, service and self-sacrifice is the spirit that alone can rule the homes and empires of the free.*[46]

## 12

# THE MAN, HIS MESSAGE, AND HIS METHODS

### "I Am Not Worth Much"

During a discussion with a candidate for the ministry, Studdert Kennedy told him that he would have to be a priest, a pastor, and a prophet. He then added, "...don't think for a moment I conform to that ideal. My ministry such as it is, might be regarded as a success; but I am conscious of continued failure."[1]

He was nationally hailed as a success yet he had his doubts. His well-known poem, just called "Woodbine Willie", reads as follows:

> *They gave me this name like their nature,*
> *Compacted of laughter and tears,*
> *A sweet that was formed of the bitter,*
> *A joke that was torn from the years.*

> *Of their travail and torture, Christ's fools,*
> *Atoning my sins with their blood,*
> *Who grinned in their agony sharing*
> *The glorious madness of God.*

> *Their name! Let me hear it – the symbol*
> *Of unpaid – unpayable debt,*
> *For the men to whom I owed God's Peace,*
> *I put off with a cigarette.*

The last verse indicates that he felt he let the soldiers down. He gave them a fag instead of comfort and hope. Feelings of despair and depression in the midst of war are understandable. But in the following years, even in the midst of crusades which attracted the applause of thousands, his sense of failure still sometimes emerged. The Reverend P. T. R. Kirk's last memory of him was

> *when at the close of a mission, he sat down still in his robes, in the clergy's vestry, almost in a state of collapse, his body shaken with sobs. He was fighting for breath in one of his attacks of asthma and trying to blurt out apologies for not doing more for the parish, making, as he said, "Such a mess of it".*[2]

In his very last book, he writes about a man asking, "What am I worth?" and he responds, "I have been there many a time and have known, God help me, I am not worth much."[3]

Geoffrey Studdert Kennedy cannot always have felt such a failure, or presumably he could not have continued his preaching and counselling. In this chapter, I will attempt to make my assessment of him. It will entail some repetition of what has gone before as I draw factors together to show him as the person he was and the person who is still relevant today.

## The Man

He was not just a public figure. He was also a husband, father, an individual with personal characteristics. Michael Grundy wrote, "Woodbine Willie had sad eyes, big ears, was only five feet six inches tall and of a generally comical appearance."[4] Purcell records that he met an elderly woman who had served in France as a nurse where she met Studdert Kennedy. She described Woodbine Willie, as she called him, "as the ugliest man she had ever met".[5] P. T. R. Kirk acknowledged about his great friend that "Kennedy's appearance was not perhaps attractive. Dark, rather tired-looking, short with thinning hair."[6]

Studdert Kennedy may well have felt deeply the remarks about his looks. In his talks he sometimes joked about his ugly face and, for instance, said, "Not only do I look like a monkey, a fact which is sadly evident on the face of it, but I frequently behave like one."[7]

Photos taken while he was a chaplain reveal a man of pleasant if not attractive appearance. Those taken in his forties do show a face that had aged, and his loss of hair did reveal more of his large ears. Nonetheless Kirk added that his physical limitations were "transformed by his attractive and whimsical smile".[8] His face was lit up by his smiles and listeners were drawn to him. The nurse cited by Purcell added that he also "had a wonderful pair of brown eyes".[9]

Purcell noticed those eyes in a wonderful portrait of Studdert Kennedy in the vestry of his former church, St Edmunds, in London. He wrote that it "brings out one feature of his physical appearance which was remarkable – the expression in his eyes. They were very large, very brown; but also… quite extraordinarily sad."[10]

The sad eyes, taken in conjunction with him being absent-minded and liable to lose possessions, have led to some calling him "a clown". As Purcell put it, despite his sadness "he was a merry man, as chockful of mischief and laughter as a clown".[11] In 2006, BBC's Radio 4 broadcast a celebration of Woodbine Willie entitled "A Clown on God's Stage". It included an actor reading, very vividly, parts of his talks, which provoked loud laughter among the audience. The implication was that his mixture of sadness and humour made him a clown in God's service.

Yes, he was sad at times, and he could clown around in small doses. In the same way that Jesus wept over Jerusalem and had a sense of humour. But these were not his outstanding characteristics. For much of the time he was overflowing with joy. A clown's main aim is to make people laugh. At times, Studdert Kennedy did have his audiences roaring with laughter but, having got their attention, he would change the mood to one of seriousness. For his main aim was not to provoke laughter but to promote a serious response to Jesus Christ and his gospel.

He was certainly a complex character. He was both conventional and unconventional. He loved the tradition of the Church of England, its set services, its repeated chants, its processions, the wearing of priestly garments. When he enlisted in the army, he did not do so as a private, as some chose to do in order to be alongside and share the life of ordinary troops. Instead, he took a commission as a chaplain, enjoyed the greater freedom of movement of officers, had a servant to look after him. After the war, he gladly accepted an appointment to be a royal chaplain.

On the other hand, he might stop a church service and invite the views of the congregation. He was known to swear violently in the midst of a talk. He shocked some church members by his readiness to discuss sex, love-making, prostitution. As Walters put it, "Not a few high placed churchmen deplored him as an ill-bred and troublesome radical."[12] He never sought high office in the church. He was glad to preach before the king but failed to turn up at a royal garden party. Emily attended and, when the king sought a reason for his absence, she explained that he had promised to speak at a church meeting and that had to come first. He never went out of his way to mix with the mighty and was always comfortable with ordinary citizens.

## The Family Man

Studdert Kennedy was a family man. Brought up in a happy and united family, he absorbed the values of love, concern, and respect that should exist between husbands and wives and parents and children. Unfortunately, even before he and Emily had children, the war separated them. Their first child, Patrick, was born during the war and, like many mothers, Emily spent much of the time looking after her child on her own. The family, extended by the births of Christopher and Michael, was united after the war in Worcester, but once Studdert Kennedy took the post with the ICF, he was parted from them for up to five days a week – excluding times together during holidays. Canon Paul Tongue, whose own father knew the Studdert Kennedys, noted, "Mrs Studdert Kennedy, and later the children too, paid a heavy price for his ministry."[13] He meant that Emily missed the closeness and support of her husband while the boys had fewer hours playing with, learning from, and relating to their father.

Andrew Studdert-Kennedy, himself a family man and Church of England minister, the Rural Dean of Marlborough, is a great admirer of his grandfather. In an interview about Studdert Kennedy's family relationships, he spoke thoughtfully about his great popularity.

> *To be in demand is very good for your ego. You can be corrupted by the popularity. It is very unusual for people not to be damaged by it. Yet in some ways, he seems not to have been. He remained very humble and self-effacing. But his heart did remain with the people. He made himself available but that could be at the expense of his family… there is something selfish about it. Those at a distance benefited from it but for those around him it was very difficult.*[14]

Andrew Studdert-Kennedy then reflected that Studdert Kennedy's insistence on continual activity stemmed from his wartime experiences:

> *When you think of what people experienced in the trenches, the kind of destruction and carnage, there must have been a strong element of post-traumatic stress which drove him. If you can retain your integrity and minister in the trenches, you can do it anywhere in the world. There is an attraction to it.*[15]

Whatever the reason, he could not stop. Andrew Studdert-Kennedy continued:

> *I went to the exhibition of Studdert Kennedy organized by Canon Paul Tongue at Worcester Cathedral. There was a register of the services he did every day. It made me feel very ambivalent about him and whether he should have been married. What a thing to impose upon people.*[16]

Paul Tongue is convinced that Studdert Kennedy did everything possible to be close to his family within the confines of his work. As rector of St Edmund's Church, he ministered there two Sundays a month. He refused to rent a flat in the area and if he had to stay overnight, it was with his friend P. T. R. Kirk who lived in London. Whenever possible on Sunday evenings, he caught the train back to Worcester and also ensured that he was always home some days in the week. On one occasion, his last meeting of a crusade was in a northern town. As soon as he could he left and was driven to Manchester where, at midnight, he caught a train to Crewe and then Worcester. He arrived in time for breakfast on the birthday of his son Patrick. There is no doubt about his deep love for his wife and sons. Significantly, in the very last paragraph in his very last book, he wrote, "I am the king of a strong kingdom of three sons. I desire above all things on earth that they may grow up fair and fine and free."[17]

Talking about Emily's reactions to her husband's frequent times away, Andrew Studdert-Kennedy commented, "I would be surprised if she did not have some resentments. I am sure she would have tried to stop him going sometimes because it was bad for him and it killed him."[18] But he added that she would never display any resentments but rather "said what a wonderful husband and father he was".[19] And that is exactly what she did do. In an interview on BBC radio some thirty-three years after her husband's death, she recorded, "He was a most devoted husband and father, good tempered and humorous. On the children's birthdays, on which he would always be here, there would be presents for them and invariably a bunch of violets for me. We had a daily correspondence which continued whenever he was away."[20] She ended by saying that their relationship was summed up in a telegram he sent which read, "Wish I could come home. The best place in the world."[21]

There is little evidence of what kind of life Emily lived after her husband died. Grundy wrote, "Some found Mrs Studdert Kennedy to be rather aloof and occasionally difficult, although these temperaments no doubt developed from years of struggling to protect her husband from those too ready to take advantage of his generosity in terms of time and money."[22] However, he received a different view from an interview with a Mrs Mary Payne who said,

"My mother and Mrs Studdert Kennedy became dear friends. After Woodbine Willie's death, Mrs Studdert Kennedy would regularly call to visit my mother at James Street in the Blockhouse."[23]

Michael Studdert-Kennedy, the youngest son of Studdert Kennedy, has communicated about his mother as follows:

> *Every year for five or six years from the time I was about eleven, she took me to see at least one Shakespeare play at Stratford-on-Avon about 25 miles from Worcester. Her brother, John, was a wealthy man, a solicitor with a house or an apartment in Leeds and a fine country house that he built himself outside Leeds. He was married to a woman, also an Emily, whom we all liked for her hearty good nature and her strong Yorkshire accent (a target of my childish snobbery and jokes), an accent oddly not shared by either John or my mother. John was rich enough to set up his only child, a son named Jack, with a fine eighteenth century Yorkshire manor, through the grounds of which ran the river Wharfe, where Jack opened and ran for many years a boys' prep school. My mother took me to visit Uncle John and Auntie Em in their country house several times, the last around 1946. John, Em and Jack would also sometimes drop in at our house in Worcester on their way to Montreux or some such Swiss resort for a skating holiday. John had the habit of giving to my mother a cheque for a hundred pounds at Christmas, together with a turkey and/or goose.*[24]

Emily Studdert Kennedy remained a loyal member of the church, helped out at the cathedral, and supported the WRVS (Women's Royal Voluntary Service). She cared devotedly for her sons. She upheld the memory of her husband, all that he stood for and all that he achieved. Just seconds before she died in 1964, she was heard to say, "Geoffrey is here, Geoffrey is here."[25] She was a remarkable part of the Studdert Kennedy partnership.

Studdert Kennedy's three sons were young when he died: Patrick was eleven, Christopher was seven, and Michael nearly two. How did they develop? There is little written about them and I rely heavily on information provided by Andrew and Michael Studdert-Kennedy. Patrick was educated at Shrewsbury School and followed his father both in being ordained and also, for a while, serving as a chaplain, although in the RAF not the army. After serving as a curate in Dudley, he became a parish priest in Somerset. He left the ministry after divorcing and remarrying. Andrew Studdert-Kennedy considers that, because of this, "he may have felt that he'd let down the family name, though that is not how others saw it."[26] Patrick died in 1988.

Christopher attended Marlborough College, then served in the forces during the Second World War before going to Oxford University. While there he became involved with the Bermondsey Boys' Club with which the university had strong links. He was ordained in 1951 and became a priest the following year. He spent his whole life ministering in the Diocese of Southwark at Bermondsey, Clapham, and Godstone where he spent twenty-five years and was finally made a Canon of Southwark Cathedral. Like his father, he chose to be a priest in deprived areas. His son Andrew Studdert-Kennedy says: "He spoke warmly of his childhood, a close relationship with Emily and a happy upbringing."[27]

Michael also went to Marlborough College and then on to Jesus College at Cambridge University where he read classics. In his late teens, he upset Emily by refusing to take Communion one Christmas on the grounds that he no longer believed in Christianity. Andrew Studdert-Kennedy commented:

> *Michael was two when his father died, so he had been brought up by his mother. His father had been incredibly famous, everybody spoke about him with bated breath but, from his point of view, he was an absent father. It was probably a difficult shadow to be brought up under.*[28]

After Cambridge, he left what he called "class-bound England" to work for the United Nations in Italy. He then settled in the USA. Andrew Studdert-Kennedy, who met up with Michael in 2011, said,

"He fled from the whole thing, he needed to escape. He reinvented himself in the US and was unable to come back when Emily died."[29] Michael asserts that his father's analysis of social problems rests too heavily on religion. He says that his books are "Rhetoric over argument, sentiment over reason, crass dismissal of anyone he disagrees with."[30] He admires his father's powerful pleas on behalf of the poor and adds that in "the spirit of my father's example I became and remained a socialist".[31] He is now a professor emeritus at Connecticut University, specializing in psychology and speech therapy. He comes over as a very humane man but very different from his father.

Studdert Kennedy loved his three sons. They reacted in different ways. Patrick and Christopher, no doubt with encouragement from Emily, were glad to follow him into the ministry. Michael, who probably had no memories of him, felt socially and emotionally suffocated by the fame of his father and broke free. The clerical link still continues through one of his grandsons, Andrew Studdert-Kennedy. Like his grandfather, he has a great concern for the socially deprived and says, "I do care a lot about the fact that the system works against the poor and in favour of the rich."[32] He is a student of both the church and capitalism, and ponders just what the church can do – if anything – to address the present economic and social crises. He adds, "The painful truth is that the Church of England is exceedingly middle class and he [his grandfather] was one of the few ministers who have been able to break out of its confines and speak for the ordinary person."[33] I suspect that Andrew Studdert-Kennedy in his role as a parish leader gives attention to the same problem. Geoffrey Studdert Kennedy would approve.

## Friendships

If the family was Studdert Kennedy's main source of personal happiness, the next was close, long-term relationships. Three stand out. First with P. T. R. Kirk, the general director of the ICF. They were work colleagues and Kirk regarded him as their main speaker and personality. There were also strong emotional bonds between them. Kirk found Studdert Kennedy to be a source of personal inspiration and regarded him as an example of how the Christian life should be lived. With his beloved Church of England experiencing low morale following the war, he saw his friend as one of its main hopes for improvement. It worked both ways. Kirk's home was always open to Studdert Kennedy, a place for a rest, a chat, and a bed. Studdert Kennedy regarded the older Kirk as his mentor and guide. For example, he discussed with Kirk whether he should continue to accept the many invitations to speak abroad and, on his advice, decided against going. Studdert Kennedy counselled many people. In his friend he had one who could counsel him.

Second, Dick Sheppard. Studdert Kennedy and Dick Sheppard had certain similarities. They were in the same age group, the former born in 1883, the latter in 1880. They both became priests and then chaplains. They were outstanding preachers with a heart for the poor. Both could be hilarious yet had a certain sadness about them. Both suffered severely from asthma, which eventually contributed to their deaths.

There were differences, however. Studdert Kennedy had a modest upbringing in terms of his family's social status and he did not attend a public boarding school. He never yearned for the company of top people. Sheppard was much more "top drawer". His clerical father was known to and served Queen Victoria. He proceeded to Marlborough College and Cambridge University. At a young age he became rector of the well-known St Martin-in–the-Fields in central London. He enjoyed the good life with meals in expensive restaurants and social events in the company of top elites.

Studdert Kennedy was the more hard-working, loath to take any breaks. His constant flow of books was such that Sheppard refused to read any more of them. Dick Sheppard had the greater organizational flair and thought up new ideas to draw people into his church and later was to catch public attention as the leader of the Peace Pledge Union. Despite the differences, they gelled and were able to relax in each other's company. Sheppard wrote of his friend, "As a companion Studdert Kennedy was a sheer delight. His laughter was a thing of joy, and his smile had a never-to-be forgotten radiance. He would sit in an armchair smoking endless cigarettes and drinking countless cups of tea, while he thrilled us with his wisdom and humour."[34] Studdert Kennedy discovered in his friend a light-heartedness which matched his own and a seriousness which encouraged him in the faith.

Third, William Temple. Temple was to become, in 1942, one of the great Archbishops of Canterbury. When he first met Studdert Kennedy, he was already ascending the ecclesiastical hierarchy. Studdert Kennedy remained at the bottom yet almost immediately they related to each other.

Their initial meeting was at a dinner in Worcester when both were in their early thirties. Thereafter they always kept in touch. Sometimes they encountered each other at large meetings in which major church concerns were discussed, sometimes in private with their wives present. Temple, despite his higher rank, was prepared to learn from his friend. He recognized his intellectual ability and admired his godliness, calling him "a prophet of social righteousness".[35] He took on board what he said about the necessity for a moral revolution before a social one could be achieved. However, after the death of Studdert Kennedy, Temple adopted a different and more political strategy for social reform, as will be explained later in this chapter.

As for Studdert Kennedy, he found in William Temple a senior church leader who respected, even loved him. They shared a devotion to the Eucharist and a belief that this service had a relevance for the wider society. They both longed for social reform as well as seeking the revival of the Church of England.

He had a number of other close friends, including the Reverend J. K. Mozley, Dr William Moore Ede of Worcester Cathedral, and the vicars of churches with whom he stayed on his preaching tours. He also maintained friendships with some parishioners in the St Paul's parish. He was friendly – if not in close friendship – with people who worked in secretarial and administrative positions at the ICF office. Andrew Studdert-Kennedy makes the astute point that "there was something very vulnerable about him which made people care about him".[36] Certainly the ICF women loved to help him when he arrived in their office having lost his money or forgotten where he was going next, or overladen with parcels for his children. Yet it was more than that, for one of the administrative personnel added, "The Holy Ghost was truly there to 'inspire and lighten with celestial fire'."[37] They recognized him as a man of God.

Clearly Studdert Kennedy had a large circle of friends. Just as clearly, they came from a very restricted group. They were all Anglican clergymen or other members of the Church of England. He had no close friends who were Roman Catholic or Nonconformist. One of his limitations was that he had little fellowship with other denominations, so his social action was mostly in the company of fellow Anglicans. It is odd that William Temple, who in the 1920s was attempting to boost ecumenism, did not move his friend in this direction.

Again, he was not on close terms with politicians of any party or with trade unionists. When governments announced legislation intended to help the unemployed and poor, Studdert Kennedy did not write about or publicly discuss it in detail. If he had nurtured friendships with political figures, he would have developed a better understanding of social policy. If he had related more closely to trade union leaders, he might have gained deeper insights into their strategies and why they sometimes resorted to strikes, which he tended to condemn.

Before leaving his personal relationships, it must be noted that his contacts with individuals, even if not close enough to be called friendships, could have long-lasting effects. While a priest at St Paul's, a choirboy listened to him intently. Years later he became a prosperous businessman respected for his help to the elderly and those in poverty, and stood for parliament in 1959. When asked in public what motivated him, he referred to "that religious spell-binder the Rev. G. A. Studdert Kennedy" and added, "When he died I resolved to dedicate myself to public service."[38] Another former member of St Paul's stated, "But for him I might have missed the path which ultimately led to my vocation to the religious life."[39]

Alfred Salter was a Quaker and a brilliant doctor who devoted his life to the poor in Bermondsey. He became a councillor, a Member of Parliament, and a minister in a Labour government. He may well have met Studdert Kennedy at meetings which called for peace. As a councillor, he wanted to transform Bermondsey into a place of beauty, with green places and flowers. His inspiration, he said, came from Woodbine Willie and he cited his words, "Be sure of this. Beauty is every bit as much a part of God as goodness."[40] And he did succeed in making Bermondsey a place with more greenery and flowers. At least one politician acknowledged a debt to Studdert Kennedy.

Some of his most telling contributions occurred when he was a chaplain. The Reverend Theodore Hardy enlisted as a chaplain at the age of fifty. He heard about Studdert Kennedy and sought him out to ask advice about how to do the job. Later Studdert Kennedy recalled some of the advice he had given:

> *Live with the men, go everywhere they go. Make up your mind you will share all their risks, and more if you can do any good. The line is the key to the whole business. Work in the very front and they will listen to you; but if you stay behind, you're wasting your time. Men will forgive you anything but lack of courage and devotion... Take a box of fags in your haversack and a great deal of love in your heart, and go up to them: laugh with them, joke with them. You can pray with them sometimes but pray for them always.*[41]

Hardy took the advice to heart. His bravery won him the Military Cross and the Victoria Cross. He wrote to the assistant chaplain general, the Reverend D. F. Carey, and asked, "Are you likely to meet or write to Studdert Kennedy soon? If so will you tell him that I have often wished I could thank him properly for that hour in your office which, more than any other in my life, has helped me in this work."[42] Soon after, in October 1918, Hardy was shot and killed. He died a hero and that one hour spent with Studdert Kennedy helped to make him so.

## The Social Evangelist

Studdert Kennedy had a range of attributes. But I believe that his greatest role in the 1920s was that of social evangelist. Evangelism is defined by the Collins English Dictionary as "the practice of spreading the Christian gospel". An evangelist is "a preacher of the Christian gospel". His evangelism, however, was wider in content than that of traditional evangelists. Dwight Moody, the American evangelist who made preaching tours of Britain, died in 1899 and Studdert Kennedy would have known of him. Like the more recent Billy Graham, such evangelists focused on being born again; that is, individuals repenting of their sins and turning to Christ for forgiveness. Studdert Kennedy certainly rejoiced at conversions to the faith, but his evangelism had a wider content. He also gave prominence to how Christianity should be lived, whether working-class people were welcomed into churches, the practice of proper sexual relationships, the ethics used by employers and employees, the relief of unemployment and poverty, and the condemnation of war. The whole gospel of how people should relate to God and society. This is social evangelism.

In the 1920s, no other Christian speaker attracted crowds like h. P. T. R. Kirk must have heard him constantly and stated that he was "able to represent God to the masses".[43] Further, he drew in many of the very population the church was most anxious to contact: the working class. They included veterans from the war, the unemployed, factory workers, dockers, miners, manual labourers. He often spoke in the open air, at the docks, in the sweat shops and factory canteens. He prophesied that, at the second coming, "He [Christ] will make for the streets... and go on with his own work."[44] He expressed this in verse in his poem "Then Will He Come".

*Then will He come – with meekness for His glory,*
*God in a workmen's jacket as before,*
*Living again the Eternal Gospel Story,*
*Sweeping the shavings from His workshop floor.*

The working class did hear him, but not just them. He longed for people from different social classes to mix and respect each other. He rejoiced when the listening audience included factory owners and factory workers, rich and poor, the educated and the uneducated.

It could be countered that he did not have to compete against TV. True, but he did have the competition of the cinema and a growing number of radio programmes. Moreover, the crowds came at a time when church attendances were continuing to decline. His popularity went against against the religious tide. Most important, his preaching did provoke a response, with numerous enquirers wanting to speak to him or his helpers. Prebendary Linsley, who helped organize some of the crusades, highlighted "his vivid personality, this loveable being that was a word that converted men. The change that he made in ordinary men's lives was the greatest factor flowing from one man to another that I have ever known."[45] George Bromby, a former leader of the unemployed who became a missioner with the ICF, was also present at meetings and commented, "He was at one with the people with whom he was speaking. I found that very often, even in a large audience, everyone had the feeling that he spoke to them."[46] Miss E. Boswell, a secretary at the ICF, recorded that many of the crowd who heard him "knew that Christ was becoming real to them through him".[47] She added that it was not just about individual conversions: "In the closing years of his life there was unemployment and poverty on a large scale. His passionate concern about this evil did much to arouse the public to get something done about it."[48]

What made Studdert Kennedy such a great social evangelist, such a compelling speaker? P. T. R. Kirk acknowledged that he was not a great orator in the sense of having a voice of charm and beauty. He said, "His voice was not the quality which woos. It was somewhat rasping, with the brogue of his Irish ancestors combining with the depth of his native Yorkshire."[49] He added that

*[his] great quality was his simplicity. Until he was better known, it was assumed that there was no depth in his*

> *reasoning, because he phrased his message in the language of the street; but it was soon evident that he was a great thinker, who puzzled out in the quiet of his own heart the immense problems of life, so that he could interpret as if he were a man without any philosophical vocabulary at all.*[50]

To be sure, Studdert Kennedy was a skilled speaker with his voice conveying both emotion and humour, with his dramatic illustrations and his pauses for silence. But his message was one of deep truth presented in a language that his hearers could understand. A shipping office worker who attended a number of meetings said that his words "seemed to me to come not from himself but from God. Indeed, Studdert Kennedy always seemed to be quite unconscious of the great crowds he attracted."[51]

Grundy aptly sums up the Studdert Kennedy he admired so much:

> *His potent mix of humour, fierce indignation of injustice, and his compelling Christian message brought flocking around him the cloth-capped and tattered prisoners of poverty and the steel helmeted and mud-splattered victims of war. The magic of his personality got to the hearts and minds of men and women, many of whom took their first steps towards the Christian faith through him.*[52]

He could have added that his social evangelism was also expressed in articles and books. Readers lapped them up. As Kenneth Woollcombe put it, "Studdert Kennedy's books sold and sold and sold. Even his poems were being re-printed in paperback in 1964. And they sold because they glowed in a dark world."[53] Given his combination of a public speaker who drew in the crowds and an author whose books were constantly reprinted, he was unmatched not only by any other clerical figure but also by any political one in the 1920s. In this respect, he was no failure.

## Promoting Social Reform

Professor Kerry Walters is typical of a number of writers when he asserts that Studdert Kennedy "was one of the most tireless and influential Christian pacifists and social reformers of the early twentieth century".[54] His contribution can be examined in three categories: his local social action, his national impact on social reform, and a shorter note on his advocacy of peace.

His concern for the poor in the parish can hardly be doubted. In Rugby, Leeds, and Worcester, he was constantly in their company. At St Paul's, he initiated the opening of a community centre. In his part-time ministry at St Edmund's in London, he was mindful of the needy within the affluent City of London and, after his death, a new block of flats, apparently financed by the Church Army, was named St Edmund's House, on which a plaque read, "…as a lasting memorial to his [Studdert Kennedy's] personal labours in housing poor families".

Despite the establishment of these two buildings, his inspiring work among poor residents was largely personal. It involved making visits to individuals to counsel and to comfort, to see them through a crisis, to provide food and clothes. This was magnificent. Its limitation was that it lacked a strategy which assessed the needs and then decided which services were required.

A contrast can be made with the Baptist minister Frederick B. Meyer.[55] Meyer was older than Studdert Kennedy but their ministries overlapped and Meyer died just twenty days before him in 1929. Meyer started as a conventional Baptist minister but gradually added a social dimension to his spiritual one. His main ministries covered two spells at Christ Church in the deprived area of North Lambeth, London, from 1892 to 1907 and from 1915 to 1920. He started by knocking on doors and relating to individuals. He soon came to important conclusions. The needs of the area were wide and varied. Young people were running wild, and there was high unemployment, poverty, drunkenness, prostitution, brothels, and loneliness. He realized that he could not tackle the problems alone or even with a few members from the church. He therefore devised a strategy. He drew local residents into the church via a social gathering for men which was short, snappy, and humorous, with tobacco rather than tea handed around. He followed with another club for their wives. The meetings also discussed the needs of the neighbourhood, and he was able to recruit and train a team of helpers who lived there. Before long, some were leaders.

The teams started youth clubs and sports activities. Prostitution and brothels proved more difficult to tackle. A hostel with resident Christian staff enabled some prostitutes to adopt a different lifestyle. Meyer then lobbied the council to enforce legal prohibitions on brothels. He was successful and persisted even when threatened with violence by the brothel owners. The money for all these advances came mainly from the pockets of the traditional worshippers whose support for Meyer's strategy was won.

Studdert Kennedy never adopted Meyer's approach; he did not set up local social services and he did not draw in local residents as leaders. If it was a limitation of his approach, it may be partly attributable to the fact that he did not stay in his parishes on a long-term basis.

Despite his successes, Meyer concluded that voluntary effort was not sufficient and that many needs could be met only by state action. He openly supported the Liberal Party, which from 1906 legislated for welfare reforms such as pensions for the elderly and benefits for the unemployed. He even spoke in favour of them at Baptist meetings when he became the national president of the Baptist Union in 1906. By contrast, Studdert Kennedy never identified with any political party. Oddly, he was sometimes referred to as a Christian socialist. Purcell makes clear that some of his clerical contemporaries sneered at him as "a Socialist".[56] Grundy wrote of him, "He readily took up the sword of Christian socialism."[57] More recently, Heaton still says that he was "a champion of Christian socialism".[58] Far from it, in his talks and in his books, as I have shown, he was a critic both of socialism and the Labour Party. It was not just Labour. He did sometimes share platforms with politicians but he never joined or openly supported any political party.

The confusion has arisen because he held aims which were similar to those of Christian socialists. He was a political radical in the sense that he too wanted major social changes. As Walters rightly points out, towards the end of the war he was calling for a new Britain, "a just, fair land where poverty, privilege and oppression have been banished".[59] So how did he attempt to promote social reform? Not by backing any political party but by preaching and writing about it. He wanted the end of poverty, the provision of decent accommodation, jobs for the unemployed. He criticized the treatment of the destitute in workhouses. He wept over the near starvation of the families of striking miners. As Purcell wrote, "He loathed our acquisitive society; he feared it; found it repulsive to live with all those status-symbols based on inequalities of possessions whether of goods or power, which most of us accept as part of the natural order."[60]

The trouble was that Studdert Kennedy failed to be precise in the nature of the changes he desired. He did not say by how much the incomes of the poor should be raised. Nor did he make clear just what income and wealth gap should exist between those at the top and the bottom. Sometimes he did attack capitalism, although he did not call it that when he raged against "the tyranny of force, vested interests, financial scheming and wire pulling... that saps the life-blood of the nation and feeds on the sorrows of the poor".[61] At other times, he appeared to defend it and certainly condemned "the vision of the great proletarian republic as a sure route to a dictatorship".[62] He wanted social change without social upheaval.

His lack of detail about the reforms for which he wanted governments to legislate made it difficult for him to comment on the changes they did or did not make and reinforced his distance from political parties. He never appeared to lobby MPs. Kirk commented that although he was fully on the side of the poor, "He did not know what was to be done to lift struggling multitudes into the degree of comfort and well-being which they ought to have as God's children. So he never entered the political arena."[63]

Another major reason for keeping politicians at arm's length was his belief that change had to emerge from morality. William

Temple, who had many discussions with Studdert Kennedy, wrote, "He never believed that the cure for economic evils was to be found by tinkering at the economic system or even by re-casting it. ... these conditions themselves are rooted and grounded in a moral state and outlook which must therefore be the first objective of attack."[64] Studdert Kennedy did not believe that a sufficient number possessed the moral values to change Britain in the direction he desired. People needed to be converted to Christian morality for, as he proclaimed, "Man's great need is moral and spiritual redemption, a Saviour who will not only change man's lot but also transform man's soul, and who perceive that only so can man's lot be changed – by the changing of his heart."[65] He drew upon the experiences and teachings of Jesus to demonstrate that it was only when rich men turned to him that they shared their money with the poor.

He saw four main outcomes of the acceptance of Christian morality:

1.  People would have a genuine concern for others. The affluent would help the poor; the poor would befriend the affluent.

2.  Rich company owners would promote improved wages and work conditions for their employees.

3.  Employees would work hard for their employers and be reluctant to strike.

4.  The multitude of transformed people would influence MPs to legislate for a more socially just society. Some MPs themselves would be transformed spiritually and take on "the desires to foster and create in our country the highest and finest kind of life".[66]

With moral transformation as the key to promoting social reform, it is not surprising that Studdert Kennedy saw the church as the main vehicle for change. As Purcell put it, "So the Church came to be for Geoffrey, with all its faults and monstrous inadequacies, the hope of the world because it was the repository and the guardian of a faith which, he came more and more to feel, alone seemed to make any sense of life."[67] Studdert Kennedy admitted that:

> *The greatest reproach of the churches is that they have so long tolerated and compromised with evil in the world. If you can really rest content while men and women sleep six and seven in a bedroom, as they do in North Kensington, for I have seen them and some in Birmingham, and even in some villages; if you can rest content while men are over-worked and under paid; if you can tolerate the waste and cruelty of war, the degradation of prostitution, you have not seen Him, you have not found your God, you are still not living but wasting life.[68]*

It followed that the church had to be revived. This explains why so many of his talks and books were aimed at churchgoers.

Further, more people had to be drawn into church because, as P. T. R. Kirk explained, Christianity had the answers "to questions of peace and war, politics, industrialisation, slums, business ethics, sex problems, sport and art".[69] The ICF crusades therefore put an emphasis on persuading more citizens to attend church in order to hear its answers.

Not least, the church had to get into the world. People might be transformed by meeting Christ within the church. But then they should meet in the places where social problems were most evident. A theme of Studdert Kennedy's at the retreats was that as Christians drew closer to Christ so they were equipped to take him to homes, schools, and workplaces.

William Temple summed up Studdert Kennedy's approach:

> *So more and more the Church came to represent for him the hope of the world, because it exists to be a society where all particular relationships are grounded in faith. But it was the church as it might be, not the church as it is, in which he found this hope.[70]*

Were the hopes of Studdert Kennedy ever realized? The church revival never came. On the contrary, the historian A. J. P. Taylor, writing of the 1920s, stated, "Not only did church-going universally decline, the dogmas of revealed religion – the Incarnation and the Resurrection – were fully accepted by only a small minority."[71] The moral revolution touched some but not vast numbers. Among the industrialists and workers who did become Christians, Purcell gives examples of some who did draw closer together in sharing and fellowship.[72] But, in general, attitudes changed little. In his last book, Studdert Kennedy regretted that the plight of the poor and unemployed was still continuing and he sadly recorded the sight of "May Day processions of workless workers past the Mayfair Hotel. It is both mean and mad."[73]

Nonetheless, he still stands out as the great Christian campaigner for social reform in the decade of the twenties. A mere priest, not a bishop, he won the ear of tens of thousands. As already illustrated in this chapter, his talks did change the lives of some individuals, who began to treat others in more Christian ways. But it is difficult to say just what he did and did not achieve in terms of improved social conditions. Some social improvements did occur in this period. The short-lived Labour government made a small increase to unemployment pay and legislated for much more council house building. Succeeding Conservative governments improved pensions for widows and elderly people and also modified the hated Poor Law by abolishing the rule of guardians and passing the Poor Law responsibilities to local authorities. Studdert Kennedy constantly called for changes but, as he tended not to specify just what was required, it is not possible to say whether he helped promote these pieces of legislation and whether he considered them sufficient. However, Kirk was quite sure that "His passionate concern for the down and outs has probably done more to arouse the public conscience than all the endless discussions can ever do."[74] It may well be that he did rouse public feelings about poverty and unemployment which, in turn, did have some effect on politicians.

If only he had lived another decade. During the 1930s, the possibility of another world war grew into a probability. A peace movement, led in particular by Dick Sheppard of the church and George Lansbury of the Labour Party, multiplied in numbers. If Studdert Kennedy had lived, he would have been in the midst of it. In 1930–31, Britain suffered a huge economic crash, with massive unemployment and financial suffering for many. Even more citizens might have been willing to take notice of Studdert Kennedy. One of the tragedies of his early death was that he never attained the height of his social reforming.

## William Temple and New Models of Social Action

The church historian Alan Wilkinson considered it a mistake for anyone in the 1920s to expect that multitudes of citizens would be converted to Christianity. A similar mistake was for church leaders interested in promoting social reform to ignore the fact that the Labour movement did include "a Christian inspiration… and it often enlisted an enthusiasm which the church did not".[75] It followed that the reformers should have worked more closely not only with Christians in the Labour movement but also with non-believing Labourites who shared some of their Christian values.

Interestingly, William Temple, although originally much influenced by Studdert Kennedy, moved to the approach of greater involvement with political parties. This was shown in his participation in the Conference on Christian Politics, Economics, and Citizenship at Birmingham in 1924. The Anglican Member of Parliament Frank Field calls it "the first of two major twentieth century Christian Socialist initiatives".[76] Its theme was that the church had to be more of an influence in shaping the values and practices of the world in matters like home life, education, poverty, industry, and property. The second initiative at Oxford in 1937 had a more international perspective, especially in regard to war and peace. To exert influence would mean combining with and cooperating with politicians and political parties – the opposite of Studdert Kennedy, who distanced himself from them.

The Second World War started in 1939 and stimulated church leaders to consider what kind of society people were fighting for. In December 1940, William Temple, still Archbishop of York, joined with other churchmen in a letter to *The Times* which called for specific social reforms of which the first was the abolition of the extreme inequalities in wealth and possessions. He also published two books which sold widely: *The Hope of a New World* and *Christianity and Social Order*.[77] In both books, he made it clear that Britain needed a vast body of people to turn to Christ. But even if this did not happen, it was still essential that Britain became a country based on Christian values. It followed that the church should engage in persuading politicians to go in this direction. On becoming Archbishop of Canterbury in 1942, he undertook a speaking campaign in which he proclaimed the foundations of a Christian society based on greater equality and fellowship. He called for the state to take over essential services and industries which private owners had regarded as their monopolies and for state family allowances as a means of abolishing child poverty. He was giving his support to the kind of welfare state which the Labour government did introduce after the war. Unfortunately, Temple did not see it, for he died in 1944.

Frank Field, in a book about his church heroes, makes a pertinent distinction between two models of social action in the New Testament. He writes, "The first is the light on the hill, beckoning and judging a fallen world. The other is the yeast which, in permeating the unleavened lump, loses its own separate identity, but has a fundamental effect on the whole process."[78] Studdert Kennedy was the light on the hill which beamed out the gospel – both spiritual and social – to a fallen world in order to transform the way people think and act. Temple, who is one of Field's heroes, admired Studdert Kennedy and rightly praised him as the great Christian voice to the world in his time. But Temple, and some of his colleagues, decided that a different approach was required: permeating political parties, which would adopt some of their policies thus spreading Christian values into the political arena. This approach had some success and probably contributed to legislation which reduced poverty and material insecurity.

## Achievements

At the end of his book, Purcell contends that sometimes Studdert Kennedy's sense of failure was partially correct and praiseworthy. He explains:

> *If Geoffrey had gone on to be in any sense a "success", as the world understands that word: the holder of dignity and position, it would somehow have done violence to that feeling about him which so many treasured so much — that he was so oddly like the Master whom he tried to serve. That being so, it would have been a pity if he had marred the picture by appearing to climb any particular ladder, or becoming respected or comfortable.*[79]

But if we judge him by Christ's standards, then he is a success, for his humility, his love of family, his identification with those he wanted to serve, his capacity for friendships, his rejection of riches and power, his willingness to serve others, are all a reflection of the Christ.

At the same time, despite his limitations, he succeeded with four main achievements. First, he was a priest who served God and people with devotion and ability. The services he conducted drew in many to truly worship God. He gave priority to the poor in his parish. He loved and was loved by many.

Second, as a chaplain in the First World War, he not only became famous as Woodbine Willie, and displayed extraordinary courage, but also, more importantly, he kept alongside ordinary soldiers and won their confidence and respect. He was frequently beside the wounded and the dying. Both in individual conversations and in addresses to hundreds of soldiers, he was able to communicate directly with them. He helped many to come to terms with profound questions about why God tolerated suffering and he showed that God still remained close to them.

Third, in the 1920s he campaigned by spoken and written word for the poor and unemployed, for the cause of social justice and for the promotion of peace. He did so as a Christian and was the greatest social evangelist of his time.

Fourth, he counselled, served, and helped many individuals. Studdert Kennedy was unusual in that he could hold the attention of thousands at a meeting and afterwards be willing to spend time with just one needy person.

He was no failure.

## Remembered and Relevant

He died in 1929. Is he still remembered and relevant today? The Reverend Kenneth Woollcombe stated, "I have studied the books about theology in the 1920s and found one reference to Studdert Kennedy."[80] He added that the main biography of William Temple also contained just one reference, although they were close friends for many years. In some ways, he is forgotten. He started no movement which bears his name. No building or church is named after him, no annual lecture is given in his name.

He may not be remembered in contemporary theological or social history books but his memory does endure. In 1962, 1994, and 2006, BBC radio programmes about him were broadcast. His name is still honoured in Worcester. In 1983, 100 years after his birth, a service of remembrance was held in the cathedral with several of his relatives in attendance. In 1987, a play entitled *Woodbine Willie: His Life and Times* was performed in Worcester with residents taking some of the parts. In 1999, Kenneth Woollcombe delivered a lecture in the cathedral to mark seventy years since his death. This was followed by a large exhibition, organized by Canon Paul Tongue, in 2009 to mark eighty years.

He is remembered by some. This is not the same as being relevant in that his example and teachings are applied to current issues. But this did happen following the participation of Britain and the USA in wars in Iraq and Afghanistan. Thousands of troops were injured, killed, traumatized by their experiences, although on a far smaller scale than the residents of the invaded countries. As in the First World War, chaplains accompanied the fighting men and attempted to help them recover and understand.

One chaplain documented his experiences in a moving, short

book. The Reverend Neal Goldsborough served as an Episcopalian chaplain in the US Navy. He was located not in Iraq but in a hospital at Camp Arifjan in Kuwait, which received wounded troops. He witnessed horrible injuries and deaths. He faced questions from combatants like "How does a God of love allow such suffering?" and turned to the writings of Studdert Kennedy – Woodbine Willie, as he always called him – for help.

He describes the face of a sergeant whose skull had been mostly blown away by a high velocity bullet. Despite the valiant efforts of the medical staff, he died. Goldsborough went to mark the sign of the cross on his brow but he no longer had a forehead. Why had God not intervened? Woodbine Willie did not have the full answer, but the chaplain took comfort from his words, "But how near the God Whom Christ revealed comes at a time like this: nearer than breathing, nearer than hands and feet, the Father of sorrow and love Who spoke through the crucified Son."[81] From them, Goldsborough realized that amidst all his sense of grief and powerlessness, God was still near.

Goldsborough also faced the death of another chaplain, who collapsed on a training run. He left a wife, three grown children, and five grandchildren. His grief was for a friend he respected, while colleagues questioned just why such a godly man should be taken. Again he turned to Woodbine Willie, who explains that Jesus himself did not escape an early death. He records that Woodbine Willie then added, "In the Risen Christ who conquered death and rose again, I find the promise and the guarantee that the moral struggle of the human race will issue in victory."[82] Goldsborough realized that God does not intervene to save the good from dying but he has intervened to ensure that death is followed by life.

The young age of some of the troops who were killed in action prompted Goldsborough to ask what happened in the next life to those who had not committed themselves to Christ. He discovered that Woodbine Willie had faced the same question when his nineteen-year-old assistant – a fine man who had no religious faith – was killed. He wrote at that time, "Well, God is greater than the churches... The river of eternal life breaks through a thousand channels and finds the soul of man."[83] His meaning was that God can come to people through voices and lessons outside of the knowledge of churches and their doctrines.

The US chaplain concludes his book by writing:

> *My year in the combat support hospital taught me to agree with Woodbine Willie. I cannot believe in a God who does not suffer with us and for us... I saw the crucified One in those courageous, broken soldiers who came to our hospital. I saw the hope of the resurrected Christ in the selfless service of our staff who worked for life and healing in the shadow of war and death.*[84]

On leaving the war zone, he took the relevance of Woodbine Willie to other chaplains.

On the eleventh day of the eleventh month of 2009, Rowan Williams, the Archbishop of Canterbury, focused on the contribution of Studdert Kennedy in a sermon to mark the passing of the First World War generation. Initially, he spoke about his work as a chaplain and how he was ready to meet the despair and questions of soldiers. He declared:

> *In all his work, in his sermons, his meditations, his astonishing poems, so many of them cast in the voice of the ordinary soldier in the trenches full of protest and apparent blasphemy, Studdert Kennedy argues against the bland problem-solving God. His commitment is to the God who is discovered in the heart of your own endurance and pain – not a solution, not a Father Christmas or fairy Godmother, but simply the one who holds your deeper self and makes it possible for you to look out on the world without loathing and despair.*[85]

The archbishop then went beyond Studdert Kennedy's contribution as a chaplain. Post First World War Britain faced economic, spiritual, and moral problems similar to those facing Britain today. Studdert Kennedy the priest, preacher, and social reformer grappled with them. He pointed out that he did not want a return to the comfortable God shaped by comfortable Christians who distanced themselves from poverty. Instead he entered into their dark lives. Rowan Williams explained, "In the darkest places you are real to yourself and one another."[86] He concluded that Studdert Kennedy's example and teaching was highly relevant to today and said:

> *You will need discipline of thinking and imagination to keep yourself real: to fight all easy answers, false gods, stifling systems... we can choose to face how vulnerable we all are and how we need to fight against our fear of one another if fear and trust and hope and love are to prevail when all is done.*[87]

The latest church leader to find the relevance of Studdert Kennedy is the Reverend Timothy Heaton in a book published in 2011 called *The Naturalist and the Christ*. It addresses two main questions: is the theory of evolution consistent with Christian teaching and – once more – why does a good God tolerate suffering? It starts with a discussion of Charles Darwin and points out that he had a knowledge, even acceptance, of Christianity and at university started a course that would have led to ordination. He abandoned this for his research which led, after many years, to his famous book *On the Origin of Species* and his theory of evolution.

Heaton is not a Creationist and sees no conflict between evolution spread over millions of years and Christianity – nor, for that matter, did Darwin. More puzzling for Heaton is the fact that evolution entailed much suffering. Darwin identified natural selection as the means by which strong animals and plants exterminated weaker ones, as did strong human beings. Nature is full of beauty and Christians sometimes see this as evidence of God at work. But nature is also about volcanoes, earthquakes, and floods which cause death and destruction.

181

At this point, Heaton draws on Studdert Kennedy who, even on a battlefield, would sometimes rejoice at sunshine and trees. He too was not a Creationist but regarded the long evolutionary process as evidence of God's power and careful planning. The cruelty of nature is a part of the process which hastens the production of resources and fruits which, in turn, enable human beings to live and flourish. Pain leads to pleasure.

Studdert Kennedy, as Heaton explains, went further than Darwin because he experienced at first hand the cruelty of war. How does this level with the almighty God of love? Heaton identifies two main responses of Studdert Kennedy. The first, to quote Heaton, is that "The power of God will not always be displayed in lifting us out of the sufferings of the world, but in enabling us to live courageously in the world as it is."[88]

The second is that the almightiness and love of God is revealed in his suffering with humankind. God in Christ lived as a common human being and suffered the pain of rejection and extreme cruelty when he was crucified. More, Studdert Kennedy insisted that God still feels pain when his creatures do so. Heaton sums up his triumphant conclusion, "To be afflicted by evil is not to be afflicted by God but to be appointed in Christ to join God's fight to conquer evil wherever it is to be found."[89]

Heaton does not claim that Studdert Kennedy is the most profound theologian in regard to the issue of suffering. He is not in the same league as the Swiss theologian Karl Barth. Nor does he consider that Studdert Kennedy's personal sufferings matched those of the German pastor Dietrich Bonhoeffer, who wrote movingly about his imprisonment before Hitler had him executed. But he does regard him as relevant because his thinking was and is expressed in talks and writings that ordinary people can grasp.

Interestingly, Heaton's book is a current Lent course for Christians. He finds Studdert Kennedy highly relevant.

Before leaving the topic of his relevance, it is worth referring to a comment by Nigel Studdert-Kennedy. He is a grandson of Geoffrey Studdert Kennedy (the son of Patrick), a retired businessman, a regular churchgoer, and an elected councillor on a district council. He wrote to me, "I suggest the question of his relevance is not whether it is for today but rather will there ever be a day when his beliefs and message will not have a relevance?"[90]

# EPILOGUE

# PERSONAL OBSERVATIONS: TOWARDS A BETTER SOCIETY

I find Studdert Kennedy relevant because, like him, I long for a better society. For me this is a society in which poverty is abolished and inequality reduced. I must explain how I came to this position. My route was less exciting than Studdert Kennedy's but I will outline it before making proposals for change.

I have one thing in common with Studdert Kennedy. I did come near to death in wartime. My first memory is of being evacuated in 1939. I returned home in time for the London Blitz. Our house was bombed, machine gunned as our family stood on the landing, severely damaged by a doodlebug with people in the street killed, and finally almost destroyed by a rocket which left my mother and brother badly injured. Then I was evacuated again. The fact that I missed so much schooling is my excuse for failing the eleven-plus examination after the war. Eventually, I did make it to grammar school. During my teens, I joined a Christian youth club whose leaders – like Studdert Kennedy – could convey Christianity to working-class youngsters.

After university, I worked as a child care officer for a local authority. I married Annette, no regrets about that, and joined the Labour Party, about which there were to be some regrets. Drawn into academic life, I became a professor of social administration at the University of Bath. I thought I had it all: high status and connections with government ministers, publications, a good salary, detached house, two cars, and a loyal wife and great children. To my surprise, I felt increasingly uneasy. Partly, I felt guilty about teaching social workers what to do while not doing it myself. More, I felt I had reduced my Christianity to a sham. I reread the Bible and met a Christ who chose to be raised by a lowly couple, who sought the company of ordinary, working-class people rather than the rich elites, who served others rather than exercising power over them. After an internal struggle and with the cooperation of Annette, I left the ivory tower and for the next thirty-plus years lived and worked in deprived areas, the kinds of places which had similarities to the poor parishes where Studdert Kennedy served.

I have known hundreds of poor people. In recent years, their plight has worsened. Since the economic crash of 2009–10, the financiers, who must take much of the blame for it, have not been punished. The poor and those on low incomes have found their material position made even worse, as the following figures and examples will show.

The official measure for child poverty is those in households with incomes below 60 per cent of the median income. In 2011, 3.8 million children were deemed poor. According to statistics from the Child Poverty Action Group, this will increase by another 600,000 by 2013.[1]

The minimum wage was raised in 2011 to £6.08 an hour. Reputable research at Loughborough University shows that this is not sufficient for the necessities of life in regard to food, clothes, furniture, travel, and leisure. It recommends a living wage of £7.20 per hour. Yet 20 per cent of all British employees earn less than this amount.[2]

Add rising unemployment and increasing homelessness, and it is not surprising that charities giving out food parcels have reappeared. Those like FareShare and the Trussell Trust report a huge rise in applications and are opening bases in new locations. A charity told me of an elderly man who wept on receiving a parcel and said that, having got food, he could spend some money on heating.

Figures from the Office of National Statistics show that the average wage increase of workers in the bottom tenth was just 0.1 per cent in 2010–11. As inflation rose more sharply, their real income declined. By contrast, the top tenth received real increases.[3] At the very top, bankers, along with the directors and chief executives of large companies, were awarded substantial increases to their existing millions. Michael Meacher MP wrote that in 2010 the total income of the 1,000 richest people in Britain rose by a massive £77.3 billion.[4] The gap between the top and bottom has widened and is now little different from that in the last years of the life of Studdert Kennedy.

The statistics make powerful reading, but I am more moved by the friends I see every week. One has been unemployed for two years and has made numerous job applications where he has competed with twenty to fifty others for the one post. He wanted to help as a washer-up at a summer camp but was told he could not go as it clashed with the day he signed on and he had to be available for work. A young man at the church I attend in Glasgow spent days walking around shops and found no vacancies. He then worked unpaid for a voluntary body for months before he was taken on at a store over Christmas. Once the new year came, he was released and is expected to work unpaid again. A woman I have known for over twenty years laboured in low-paid posts until her health declined. In all that time, she only went on holiday once and that was when I raised some money to enable her and her children to go to Butlins. Nearby is a family I visit who have always lived in a damp flat and have no savings to meet any emergencies. Compare these people with the highly paid who live in substantial homes, who possess large bank balances, who spend freely on clothes and restaurants, whose children have large gardens and numerous toys, and who annually enjoy luxurious holidays abroad. I share the anger that Studdert Kennedy felt about such unjust differences.

My anger about these social differences rests on two grounds. First, as a Christian I believe that God created all people of equal worth and so, as far as possible, the resources, opportunities, and responsibilities of God's world should be distributed among the many not the few. Jesus never sought riches, he instructed his followers to help the poor, warned of the dangers of greed, and forbade them to accumulate possessions. Studdert Kennedy too was familiar with this teaching.

Second, I have long perceived that poverty is associated with underachievement at school, getting unskilled jobs, inadequate housing, debt, and premature death. More recently, I read of the shocking outcomes of inequality. In 2009, Professors Richard Wilkinson and Kate Pickett published their study of 200 pieces of reputable research. Entitled *The Spirit Level: Why More Equal Societies Almost Always Do Better*, it compared unequal countries like the USA and Britain, where the top 20 per cent earned seven to nine times as much as the bottom 20 per cent, with more equal countries like Finland, Sweden, and Norway, where the top earned only two to three times as much.[5] The unequal countries scored higher on almost all social problems, including physical and mental ill health, violence, teenage pregnancies, child abuse, desertion by fathers, imprisonment, and unemployment. They argued that the more equal places did better because personal greed was not such a driving force and because people in different occupations were more likely to live in the same neighbourhoods and to respect each other. A sense of community rathar than division prevailed. In short, greater equality made for a better society.

The case for the abolition of poverty and the spread of greater equality rests both on Christian values and a more general belief that it is right to pursue a more contented and united country. But who will promote the case? The obvious body seems to be the Labour Party. After all, Keir Hardie, the main founder of the party, was an egalitarian who said, "Socialism implies the inherent equality of all human beings."[6] When William Temple and his colleagues pushed for social reforms, they found willing listeners in a Labour Party which was already planning the welfare state it was to bring into operation after the war. It was the party I joined fifty years ago, precisely because I believed it would attack poverty and social inequality. But that Labour Party is no more. In his exhaustive, and sometimes exhausting, book, Andrew Rawnsley brilliantly details the rise of New Labour under the leadership of Tony Blair, who loved money so much that "the super-rich provoked him into expressions of awe and jealousy".[7] Blair was succeeded by Gordon Brown and then Ed Miliband.

Certainly, while in power the party made some improvements to social services but it awarded numerous titles and peerages to financiers for services to banking, but not one for services to equality. Some Labour MPs, whom I know and respect, still push for radical reforms. But generally, the abolition of poverty and the end of inequality are no longer priorities.

At the time of writing, the country is governed by a coalition of Conservatives and Liberal Democrats with a cabinet which includes seventeen millionaires. The three major parties are now much the same in social composition. Not my judgement, rather that of a significant but ignored report by the Speaker of the House of Commons issued in 2010. Compiled by sixteen MPs, advised by experts, it found that the number of MPs from working-class backgrounds had declined sharply even in Labour. Of all MPs, 89 per cent had been to university, with 27 per cent drawn from the tiny minority of the population that attends Oxbridge. It stated, "There is little sense that members understand or share the life experiences of their constituents."[8] Labour as well as the other parties is distanced from citizens who struggle to make ends meet.

Who can make the case for a more equal society? This is where Studdert Kennedy is still relevant. I have seen it as one of his limitations that he failed to mix with politicians in order to learn about legislation. Yet it also gave him a sturdy independence not only from politicians but also from financiers, the wealthy, and others who might wish to influence what he said and wrote. The body he did identify with was the Church of England. But he never swayed the whole of that church to his side. It had bishops who despised his radical views. It had wealthy members who saw him as a threat to their riches. Moreover, he never drew in churches from other denominations. When Temple later popularized his call for reform, he did not claim to have the whole of the church behind him.

Today the Church of England – along with other churches – is numerically even smaller than in the 1920s. Further, it is still not united over the issues of poverty and inequality. It does have leaders who speak for the poor, although less vehemently against the rich who donate to their churches. Others blame the poor for their own poverty. An example of division concerns the occupation of the area outside of St Paul's Cathedral in 2011 by protesters against the greed of financiers. Within St Paul's some clerics backed the protesters while others supported moves to evict them.

I fleetingly considered proposing a new Christian agency to concentrate just on campaigning for the end of poverty and inequality, but no, there are already numerous church and Christian agencies. Christians from various denominations (and no denomination) support the likes of Church Action on Poverty, which does excellent work despite its struggle for funds. Others are active in secular and Christian groups in the front line. Writing about the Trussell Trust, which gives out 100,000 emergency food parcels a year, Felicity Lawrence says that the work is largely undertaken by unpaid, local Christians who are unfailingly caring and sensitive.[9] I ask them to go the extra mile not by joining another organization but by trying to influence local opinion, speaking to friends and relatives, writing to the press and MPs, and raising the matter in their churches. If only we talked about the needs of the poor and the unequal as much as we do about sport, music, and TV.

The essence of our talking, lobbying, and writing is fourfold. First, our case is that poverty and gross inequality is un-Christian. Second, we should not talk vaguely but specify what we believe should be the minimum income under which no individual should fall and what should be the maximum earnings which no one should exceed. Third, we should be prepared to criticize our own rich. Tony Blair is a Christian who undertakes worthy work to facilitate understanding between different faiths. But he is also a multi-millionaire in a society where many cannot afford a decent lifestyle and the owner of a huge property portfolio in a land where tens of thousands are homeless. Jesus never condemned the poor, but he did criticize the wealthy. Fourth, we should make clear that the changes we want are for the good of all and will lead to a more contented, more healthy, more united society.

So I am not seeking a powerful, well-connected pressure group with a chief executive stuffing £150,000 a year into his/her pockets, and with polished media experts to win the support of celebrities. Instead, I want to encourage Christians – and others who share their values – to speak, argue, and lobby. No chance of making an impact? Studdert Kennedy often stressed the upside-down nature of Christianity. Jesus had little money, not even a room, lacked political friends, never sought the approval of the royals, and was despised by the powerful. Yet somehow his strength was in weakness, his achievements in his sufferings. And the extra-mile participants may establish that their views are not those of a minority. A recent poll revealed that 78 per cent "would support government action to reduce the gap between high and low incomes".[10]

## Living the Life

Studdert Kennedy was no failure. He was an extraordinary voice on behalf of the poor and for peace. Most of us cannot be a national figure like him. Yet there is something else about him which, perhaps, we can emulate. He lived the life; that is, his everyday actions and attitudes were in keeping with his principles and beliefs. As a Christian, he considered it wrong that some should live in luxury and others in penury. He disliked the way in which the wealthy distanced themselves from fellow human beings who happened to have low incomes and overcrowded accommodation. Consequently, as a priest he served only in poor parishes, where he spent much time in the houses squashed into back-to-back terraces. Some evenings he would laugh and sing in the local pub before going to sit with the sick and dying in their cold homes. He spoke or wrote about the humanity and humility of the Son of God who sought the company of fishermen, who welcomed the presence of prostitutes and accepted the approaches of aliens; that is, those from foreign countries. He was not an inverted snob who shunned the privileged. He was on close terms with William Temple and Dick Sheppard and others in their comfortable positions. But these friendships did not lead to him abandoning friends who were much lower down the social scale. And he did not use their social influence as a means to obtain honours or to climb the social hierarchy.

He saw the hunger, cold, and ill health associated with poverty. He responded by giving away his money, clothes, and possessions to those in need. He was not concerned about the trappings of money. He cared little about the cut of his clothes. He travelled extensively by train but never, as far as I can ascertain, did he go first class. Monetary greed seemed entirely absent from his character. He never sought a high salary, and the considerable amount he made from his books he gave away.

No lover of money or status, content with the company of all kinds of people, humble in appearance and practice. Certainly he had faults and limitations and some have been mentioned in this book. But he deserves the judgement which P. T. R. Kirk made about him: "He taught by example as well as by precept. He had the human touch if ever a man had it."[11]

I hope that some Christians and others committed to the well-being of those in poverty and inequality will also choose lifestyles that reflect their values and which could be a power for good. For a start, living modestly. This does not mean that those in top jobs should leave them. Rather it is about being satisfied with a portion of their salary and giving the surplus to people in need or to the agencies which help them. We can reduce our spending on expensive cars, huge TVs, numerous electronic gadgets, the latest fashions in clothes, classy restaurants, and expensive holidays abroad. Any savings can be used in the way that Studdert Kennedy was generous to others.

## Dwelling in Cheaper Areas

I have friends who have deliberately moved into very deprived neighbourhoods. I am not suggesting we all do likewise. I am asking that, instead of enjoying the benefits of highly priced houses, we should consider relocating to cheaper, less fashionable places. Yes, it will mean financial loss, as our home will not increase in value as do those in sought-after areas. But it will put us closer to people at the hard end of society, enable us to join with them in improving local schools and the community, allow us to support neighbourhood shops, and open our eyes and minds to what it is like to survive on an income that is barely adequate.

## Using Our Money Ethically

We can decide to lodge and invest our savings in bodies which do not stimulate greed and inequality. The Co-operative Bank, unlike the major High Street banks, is based on ethical principles. For instance, it refuses to trade with companies that enrich their shareholders by trading in arms. It does not pay huge bonuses and did not indulge in the high risk loans by which other banks contributed to the credit crisis. It has not shed thousands of jobs. Co-operative food shops are a wing of the growing co-op movement but remain small enough to be part of their local communities. Profits are distributed to members via the famous divi. Members can also vote and participate in committees which shape policies. As for me, instead of shopping in the huge supermarkets, I go daily to the local co-op, I also insure with the co-op, use its pharmacy and, when I die, will be buried by it – with my wife donating the divi to charity.

Not just the co-op. We can shop with firms owned by their workers. We can invest with mutual building societies. We can join credit unions, many of which make low interest loans to people on low incomes whom the big banks don't accept. As a result, the borrowers do not have to resort to loan sharks.

These practices are important. They challenge the evils of greed and materialism. They make the case for greater equality. They reduce the social divisions within society. They demonstrate that commercial cooperation which puts communal good before selfishness is an alternative to the worst kinds of competition. If the participants in modest living multiply in number, they may even exert pressure on governments to attempt to abolish poverty and to create the good society in which citizens are bound in fellowship rather than separated by huge differences in income, wealth, and possessions.

Andrew Studdert-Kennedy said of his grandfather, "He was one of those very unusual people who did practise what he preached. He was genuine."[12] We can follow in his footsteps.

# NOTES

Worcester Cathedral Archives contain a number of useful papers, letters, and articles about Studdert Kennedy. However, they are not indexed and often not dated, so reference to any of them is simply given as "Worcester Cathedral Archives". Information was obtained from the recordings of two BBC radio programmes. One broadcast in 1962 was entitled "The Way of Life" and the other in 2006 was "A Clown on God's Stage". Information from them is referred to as "BBC Radio programme" followed by the appropriate year. Material from an important interview with Andrew Studdert-Kennedy in 2011 is referred to as "Interview with Andrew Studdert-Kennedy". An informative email exchange with Michael Studdert-Kennedy in 2012 is referred to as "Personal communication with Michael Studdert-Kennedy", another with Nigel Studdert-Kennedy in 2012 as "Personal communication with Nigel Studdert-Kennedy".

## 1. Childhood and Education, 1883–1904

1. Geoffrey A. Studdert Kennedy, *Lies*, London, Hodder & Stoughton, 1919, pp. 109–10.

2. Benjamin Seebohm Rowntree, *A Study of Town Life*, London, Macmillan, 1901.

3. Iain Gazeley and Andrew Newell, *Poverty in Britain in 1904*, Brighton, University of Sussex, 2007.

4. Quoted in J. K. Mozley, "Home Life and Early Years of His Ministry" in J. K. Mozley (ed.), *G.A. Studdert Kennedy by his Friends*, London, Hodder & Stoughton, 1929, p. 14.

5. *Ibid.*, p. 37.

6. *Ibid.*, p. 33.

7. *Ibid.*, p. 15.

8. Geoffrey A. Studdert Kennedy, *The Wicket Gate*, London, Hodder & Stoughton, 1923, pp. 11–12.

9. Mozley, "Home Life and Early Years of His Ministry", pp. 30–31.

10. Quoted in Mozley, "Home Life and Early Years of His Ministry", p. 45.

11. Mozley, "Home Life and Early Years of His Ministry", pp. 31–32.

12. Michael Grundy, *A Fiery Glow in the Darkness: Woodbine Willie, Padre and Poet*, Worcester, Osborne Books, 1997, p. 13.

13. Quoted in Mozley, "Home Life and Early Years of His Ministry", pp. 22–23.

14. Mozley, "Home Life and Early Years of His Ministry", p. 17.

## 2. Into the Church, 1905–14

1. William Purcell, *Woodbine Willie, a Study of Geoffrey Studdert Kennedy*, London and Oxford, Mowbray Religious Reprints, 1982 (first published 1962), p. 42.

2. *Ibid.*, p. 45.

3. *Ibid.*, p. 44.

4. J. K. Mozley, "Home Life and Early Years of His Ministry", in J. K. Mozley (ed.), *G. A. Studdert Kennedy by his Friends*, London, Hodder & Stoughton, 1929, p. 47.

5. *Ibid.*, p. 49.

6. Alan Wilkinson, *The Church of England and the First World War*, London, SPCK, 1978, p. 5.

7. Sir Robert Ensor, *England 1870–1914*, Oxford, Clarendon Press, reprinted 1966, p. 305.

8. Mozley, "Home Life and Early Years of His Ministry", p. 49.

9. Purcell, *Woodbine Willie*, pp. 46–47.

10. Mozley, "Home Life and Early Years of His Ministry", p. 53.

11. *Ibid.*, pp. 54–55.

12. *Ibid.*, p. 51.

13. Purcell, *Woodbine Willie*, p. 55.

14. *Ibid.*, p. 54.

15. Bob Holman, *Good Old George: The Life of George Lansbury*, Oxford, Lion, 1990, p. 43.

16. Mozley, "Home Life and Early Years of His Ministry", pp. 60–61.

17. Worcester Cathedral Archives.

18. Mozley, "Home Life and Early Years of His Ministry", p. 57.

19. *Ibid.*, p. 72.

20. *Ibid.*

21. BBC Radio programme, 1962.

22. Mozley, "Home Life and Early Years of His Ministry", pp. 74–75.

23. Worcester Cathedral Archives.

24. *Ibid.*

## 3. Worcester and War, 1914–16

1. Christopher Hart, *The History and Architecture of St Paul's Church Worcester* (pamphlet), Worcester, St Paul's Church, 1995, p. 4.

2. P. T. R. Kirk, "Studdert Kennedy: I. C. F. Crusader", in J. K. Mozley (ed.), *G. A. Studdert Kennedy by his Friends*, London, Hodder & Stoughton, London, 1929, p. 181.

3. Paul Tongue, *Father Geoffrey Studdert Kennedy, Parish Priest, Woodbine Willie: A Short Introduction* (pamphlet), Worcester, Worcester Cathedral, 2009, p. 5.

4. Worcester Cathedral Archives.

5. Michael Grundy, *A Fiery Glow in the Darkness: Woodbine Willie, Padre and Poet*, Worcester, Osborne Books, 1997, p. 13.

6. Hart, *St Paul's Church Worcester*, p. 2.

7. BBC Radio programme, 1962.

8. William Moore Ede, "His Life in Worcester", in J. K. Mozley (ed.), *G. A. Studdert Kennedy by his Friends*, London, Hodder & Stoughton, 1929, p. 90.

9. Tongue, *Father Geoffrey Studdert Kennedy*, p. 3.

10. Moore Ede, "His Life in Worcester", p. 90.

11. Grundy, *A Fiery Glow in the Darkness*, p. 24.

12. Gary Sheffield, *The First World War: The Road to War* (pamphlet), London, The Guardian, 2008, pp. 4–9.

13. A. J. P. Taylor, *English History 1914–1945*, London, Pelican Books, reprinted 1987, pp. 46–47.

14. Worcester Cathedral Archives.

15. *Ibid.*

16. Moore Ede, "His Life in Worcester", p. 100.

17. Worcester Cathedral Archives.

18. *Ibid.*

19. *Ibid.*

20. *Ibid.*

21. Taylor, *English History 1914–1945*, p. 93.

22. Geoffrey A. Studdert Kennedy, *Rough Talks by a Padre*, London, Hodder & Stoughton, 1918, p. 17.

23. Studdert Kennedy, *Rough Talks by a Padre*, p. 20.

24. *Ibid.*, pp. 21–22.

25. William Purcell, *Woodbine Willie, a Study of Geoffrey Studdert Kennedy*, London and Oxford, Mowbray Religious Reprints, 1982 (first published 1962), p.121.

## 4. The Wandering Preacher, 1916–17

1. Alan Wilkinson, *The Church of England and the First World War*, London, SPCK, 1978, p. 76.

2. Worcester Cathedral Archives.

3. Kerry Walters (ed.), *After War, Is Faith Possible? G. A. Studdert Kennedy, "Woodbine Willie." An Anthology*, Cambridge, The Lutterworth Press, 2008, p. 12.

4. Geoffrey A. Studdert Kennedy, *Rough Talks by a Padre*, London, Hodder & Stoughton, 1918, pp. 22, 35, 173.

5. Bob Holman, *Keir Hardie: Labour's Greatest Hero?* Oxford, Lion Hudson, 2010, p. 176.

6. Norman Lowe, *Mastering Modern British History*, London, Macmillan, 1989, 2nd edition, pp. 410–11.

7. Studdert Kennedy, *Rough Talks by a Padre*, p. 60.

8. *Ibid.*, pp. 70–71.

9. Wilkinson, *The Church of England and the First World War*, p. 99.

10. Studdert Kennedy, *Rough Talks by a Padre*, p. 27.

11. *Ibid.*, p. 28.

12. Walters, *After War, Is Faith Possible?*, p. 10.

13. Richard Tawney, *The Attack and Other Papers*, Nottingham, Spokesman, 1981, p. 26.

14. Studdert Kennedy, *Rough Talks by a Padre*, p. 112.

15. *Ibid.*, p. 107.

16. *Ibid.*, p. 106.

17. *Ibid.*, p. 102.

18. *Ibid.*, pp. 114–15.

19. *Ibid.*, p. 31.

20. *Ibid.*, pp. 31–32.

21. *Ibid.*, p. 123.

22. *Ibid.*, p. 126.

23. *Ibid.*, p. 138.

24. *Ibid.*, 163–64.

25. William Purcell, *Woodbine Willie, a Study of Geoffrey Studdert Kennedy*, London and Oxford, Mowbray Religious Reprints, 1982 (first published 1962), p.105.

26. Walters, *After War, is Faith Possible?*, p. 10.

27. Studdert Kennedy, *Rough Talks by a Padre*, p. 151.

28. Geoffrey A. Studdert Kennedy, *The Hardest Part*, London, Hodder & Stoughton, 1918, p. 6.

29. *Ibid.*, p. viii.

30. George Lansbury, *Your Part in Poverty*, London, Allen and Unwin, p. 100.

## 5. *Rough Rhymes*, 1917–18

1. Worcester Cathedral Archives.

2. Malcolm Brown, "After Ninety Years", in John Brophy and Eric Partridge (eds), *The Daily Telegraph Dictionaries of Tommies' Songs and Slang 1914–1918*, London, Frontline Books, 2008, p. vii.

3. William Purcell, *Woodbine Willie, a Study of Geoffrey Studdert Kennedy*, London and Oxford, Mowbray Religious Reprints, 1982 (first published 1962), p. 130.

4. *Ibid.*, p. 126.

## 6. On the Front Line Again, 1917–18

1. J. H. Johnson, *Stalemate! The Real Story of Trench Warfare*, London, Rigel Publications, 1995, p. 127.

2. "The First World War Diaries of a Black Soldier", *The Herald*, 18 May 2011.

3. Geoffrey A. Studdert Kennedy, *The Hardest Part*, London, Hodder & Stoughton, 1918, pp. 3–4.

4. *Ibid.*, pp. 8–9.

5. *Ibid.*, pp. 9–11.

6. *Ibid.*, pp. 12–13.

7. *Ibid.*, p. 14.

8. *Ibid.*, p. 29.

9. *Ibid.*, p. 68.

10. *Ibid.*, p. 154–55.

11. *Ibid.*, p. 157.

12. D. F. Carey, "Studdert Kennedy: War Padre", in J. K. Mozley (ed.), *G. A. Studdert Kennedy by his Friends*, London, Hodder & Stoughton, 1929, pp. 142–43.

13. *The London Gazette*, 16 August 1917.

14. Michael Grundy, *A Fiery Glow in the Darkness: Woodbine Willie, Padre and Poet*, Worcester, Osborne Books, 1997, p. 48.

15. William Purcell, *Woodbine Willie: A Study of Geoffrey Studdert Kennedy*, London, Mowbray Religious Reprints, 1982 (first published 1962), p. 120.

16. Worcester Cathedral Archives.

17. *Ibid.*

18. *Ibid.*

19. *Ibid.*

20. *Ibid.*

21. *Ibid.*

22. *Ibid.*

23. *Ibid.*

24. Carey, "Studdert Kennedy: War Padre", pp. 128–29.

25. *Ibid.*, p. 129.

26. Worcester Cathedral Archives.

27. A. J. P. Taylor, *English History 1914–1945*, London, Pelican Books, reprinted 1987, p. 157.

28. Worcester Cathedral Archives.

29. Peter Fiennes, *To War With God: The Army Chaplain Who Lost*

*His Faith*, Edinburgh and London, Mainstream Publishing, 2011, pp. 230–31.

30. Alan Wilkinson, *The Church of England and the First World War*, London, SPCK, 1978, p. 110.

31. *Ibid.*

32. C. E. Montague, *Disenchantment*, London, Chatto and Windus, 1922, p. 73.

33. Fiennes, *To War With God*, p. 89.

34. Alan Hanbury-Sparrow, "Front Line Chaplain", in Kenneth Brill (ed.), *John Groser: East End Priest*, London and Oxford, Mowbrays, 1971, pp. 27–28.

35. Wilkinson, *The Church of England and the First World War*, p. 145.

36. Kenneth Woollcombe, "A Fiery Glow in the Darkness: The Influence of Studdert Kennedy on the Thinking of the Church" (public lecture), Worcester, Worcester Cathedral, 1997, p. 3.

37. Purcell, *Woodbine Willie*, p. 115.

## 7. *The Hardest Part*, 1918

1. Geoffrey A. Studdert Kennedy, *The Hardest Part*, London, Hodder & Stoughton, 1918, pp. xx–xxi.

2. *Ibid.*, p. 10.

3. *Ibid.*, p. 185.

4. D. F. Carey, "Studdert Kennedy: War Padre", in J. K. Mozley (ed.), *G. A. Studdert Kennedy by his Friends*, London, Hodder & Stoughton, 1929, p. 154.

5. Studdert Kennedy, *The Hardest Part*, p. 112.

6. *Ibid.*, p. 127.

7. *Ibid.*, p. 117.

8. *Ibid.*, p. 133.

9. *Ibid.*, p. 94.

10. *Ibid.*, p. 95.

11. *Ibid.*

12. *Ibid.*, pp. 101–102.

13. *Ibid.*, p. 105.

14. *Ibid.*, p. 107.

15. *Ibid.*, p. 52.

16. J. K. Mozley, "Home Life and Early Years of His Ministry", in J. K. Mozley (ed.), *G. A. Studdert Kennedy by his Friends*, p. 65.

17. Studdert Kennedy, *The Hardest Part*, pp. 14–15.

18. *Ibid.*, p. 27.

19. *Ibid.*

20. Studdert Kennedy, *The Hardest Part*, p. 28.

21. *Ibid.*, pp. 70, 72.

22. *Ibid.*, pp. 70–71.

23. *Ibid.*, p. 93.

24. *Ibid.*, p. 89.

25. *Ibid.*, pp. 67–68.

26. *Ibid.*, p. 80.

27. *Ibid.*, p. 81.

28. William Purcell, *Woodbine Willie: A Study of Geoffrey Studdert Kennedy*, London and Oxford, Mowbray Religious Reprints, 1982 (first published 1962), p. 146.

## 8. From Local Priest to National Preacher, 1919–21

1. Worcester Cathedral Archives.

2. Geoffrey A. Studdert Kennedy, *Lies*, London, Hodder & Stoughton, 1919, p. 114.

3. Michael Grundy, *A Fiery Glow in the Darkness: Woodbine Willie, Padre and Poet*, Worcester, Osborne Books, 1997, p. 66.

4. *Ibid.*, p. 65.

5. *Ibid.*

6. *Ibid.*, p. 66.

7. Worcester Cathedral Archives.

8. *Ibid.*

9. K. Walters (ed.), *After War, Is Faith Possible? G. A. Studdert Kennedy "Woodbine Willie." An Anthology*, Cambridge, The Lutterworth Press, 2008, p. 15.

10. C. E. Montague, *Disenchantment*, London, Chatto and Windus, 1922, pp. 200–201.

11. *Ibid.*, p. 200.

12. William Purcell, *Woodbine Willie: A Study of Geoffrey Studdert Kennedy*, London and Oxford, Mowbray Religious Reprints, 1982 (first published 1962), p. 155.

13. Richard Overy, *The Morbid Age*, London, Penguin Books, 2010, p. 16.

14. Donald Hankey, *A Student in Arms*, London, Alan Melrose Ltd, 1918, p. 100.

15. Alan Wilkinson, *The Church of England and the First World War*, London, SPCK, 1978, p. 230.

16. William Moore Ede, "His Life in Worcester", in J. K. Mozley (ed.), *G. A. Studdert Kennedy by his Friends*, London, Hodder & Stoughton, 1929, p. 107.

17. Worcester Cathedral Archives.

18. *Ibid.*

19. *Ibid.*

20. *Ibid.*

21. *Ibid.*

22. *Ibid.*

23. *Ibid.*

24. *Ibid.*

25. *Ibid.*

26. *Ibid.*

27. *Ibid.*

28. *Ibid.*

29. *Ibid.*

30. Grundy, *A Fiery Glow in the Darkness*, p. 66.

31. Studdert Kennedy, *Lies*, p. 13.

32. *Ibid.*, p. 25.

33. *Ibid.*, p. 26.

34. *Ibid.*, p. 30.

35. *Ibid.*, p. 41.

36. *Ibid.*, p. 43.

37. Ross Terrill, *R. H. Tawney and His Times*, London, Andre Deutsch, 1974, p. 136.

38. Studdert Kennedy, *Lies*, p. 40.

39. *Ibid.*, p. 116.

40. *Ibid.*, p. 117.

41. *Ibid.*, p. 116.

42. Purcell, *Woodbine Willie*, p.167.

43. Walters, *After War, Is Faith Possible?*, p. 16.

44. Kenneth Woollcombe, "A Fiery Glow in the Darkness: The Influence of Studdert Kennedy on the Thinking of the Church" (public lecture), Worcester, Worcester Cathedral, 1997, p. 4.

45. Geoffrey A. Studdert Kennedy, *Food for the Fed-Up*, London, Hodder & Stoughton, 1921, p. 1.

46. *Ibid.*, p. 7.

47. *Ibid.*, p. 29.

48. *Ibid.*, p. 28.

49. *Ibid.*, p. 45.

50. *Ibid.*, p. 107.

51. *Ibid.*, p. 53.

52. *Ibid.*, p. 310.

53. Purcell, *Woodbine Willie*, p. 165.

54. *Ibid.*, p. 169.

55. *Ibid.*, p. 166.

56. Walters, *After War, Is Faith Possible?*, p. 16.

57. Studdert Kennedy, *Food for the Fed-Up*, p. 77.

58. Geoffrey Studdert Kennedy, *Democracy and the Dog Collar*, London, Hodder & Stoughton, 1921, p. 4.

59. *Ibid.*, p. 4.

60. *Ibid.*, p. 7.

61. *Ibid.*, p. 26.

62. *Ibid.*, pp. 198–99.

63. *Ibid.*, p. 107.

64. *Ibid.*, p. 47.

65. *Ibid.*, p. 53.

66. *Ibid.*, p. 139.

67. *Ibid.*, pp. 34–35.

68. *Ibid.*, p. 78.

69. Walters, *After War, Is Faith Possible?*, p. 18.

70. Worcester Cathedral Archives.

71. *Ibid.*

72. *Ibid.*

73. *Ibid.*

74. Grundy, *A Fiery Glow in the Darkness*, p. 70.

## 9. The National Figure, 1921–29

1. ICF website, http://www.icf-online.org/.

2. *Ibid.*

3. Gerald Studdert-Kennedy, *Dog-Collar Democracy: The Industrial Christian Fellowship 1919–1929*, London, Macmillan Press, 1982, p. 172.

4. David Thomson, *England in the Twentieth Century, 1914–1963*, Harmondsworth, Penguin Books, reprinted 1978, p. 120.

5. Graham Dale, *God's Politicians*, London, HarperCollins, 2000, p. 18.

6. Studdert-Kennedy, *Dog-Collar Democracy*, p. 96.

7. *Ibid.*, p. 4.

8. A. J. P. Taylor, *English History 1914–1945*, London, Pelican Books, reprinted 1987, p. 226.

9. William Purcell, *Woodbine Willie: A Study of Geoffrey Studdert Kennedy*, London and Oxford, Mowbray Religious Reprints, 1982 (first published 1962), p. 203.

10. *Ibid.*, pp. 204–205.

11. P. T. R. Kirk, "Studdert Kennedy: I. C. F. Crusader", in J. K. Mozley (ed.), *G. A. Studdert Kennedy by his Friends*, London, Hodder & Stoughton, 1929, pp. 178–79.

12. Alan Johnston, "On the Road", *New Socialist*, January 1985.

13. Studdert-Kennedy, *Dog-Collar Democracy*, p. 157.

14. Purcell, *Woodbine Willie*, p. 196.

15. Worcester Cathedral Archives.

16. *Ibid.*

17. *Ibid.*

18. *Ibid.*

19. *Ibid.*

20. *Ibid.*

21. Interview with Andrew Studdert-Kennedy.

22. BBC Radio programme, 1962.

23. Studdert-Kennedy, *Dog-Collar Democracy*, p. 3.

24. Alan Wilkinson, *Dissent or Conform? War, Peace and the English Churches 1900–1945*, London, SCM Press, 1986, p. 146.

25. Michael Walsh (ed.), *Dictionary of Christian Biography*, London and New York, Continuum Press, 2001, p. 641.

26. Studdert-Kennedy, *Dog-Collar Democracy*, pp.159–60.

27. *Ibid.*, p. 163.

28. *Ibid.*

29. *Ibid.*, pp. 3–4.

30. *Ibid.*, p. 3.

31. P. T. R. Kirk, "Studdert Kennedy: I. C. F. Crusader", p. 182.

32. BBC Radio programme, 1962.

## 10. More Books Including a Novel, 1923–29

1. Geoffrey A. Studdert Kennedy, *The Wicket Gate*, London, Hodder & Stoughton, 1923, p. 11, quoting from *Pilgrim's Progress*.

2. *Ibid.*, p. 52.

3. *Ibid.*, p. 222.

4. *Ibid.*, p. 57.

5. *Ibid.*, p. 73.

6. Michael Grundy, *A Fiery Glow in the Darkness: Woodbine Willie, Padre and Poet*, Worcester, Osborne Books, 1997, p. 59.

7. Studdert Kennedy, *The Wicket Gate*, p. 86.

8. Gerald Studdert-Kennedy, *Dog-Collar Democracy: The Industrial Christian Fellowship 1919–1929*, London, Macmillan Press, 1982, p. 136.

9. Geoffrey A. Studdert Kennedy, *The Word and the Work*, London, Longmans, Green & Co., 1925, p. 5.

10. Studdert-Kennedy, *Dog-Collar Democracy*, p. 106.

11. Studdert Kennedy, *The Word and the Work*, p. 61.

12. *Ibid.*, p. 65.

13. Geoffrey A. Studdert Kennedy, *I Pronounce Them: A Story of Man and Wife*, London, Hodder & Stoughton, 1927, p. 7.

14. *Ibid.*, p. 11.

15. *Ibid.*, p. 13.

16. *Ibid.*, p. 155.

17. *Ibid.*, p. 191.

18. *Ibid.*, p. 316.

19. William Temple, "Studdert Kennedy: The Man and His Message", in J. K. Mozley (ed.), *G. A. Studdert Kennedy by his Friends*, London, Hodder & Stoughton, 1929, pp. 206–207.

20. William Purcell, *Woodbine Willie: A Study of Geoffrey Studdert Kennedy*, London and Oxford, Mowbray Religious Reprints, 1982 (first published 1962), p. 209.

21. Geoffrey A. Studdert Kennedy, *The Warrior, the Woman and the Christ*, London, Hodder & Stoughton, 1928, p. 302.

22. *Ibid.*, p. 304.

23. *Ibid.*, p. 46.

24. *Ibid.*, p. 74.

25. Purcell, *Woodbine Willie*, p. 208.

26. Studdert Kennedy, *The Warrior, the Woman and the Christ*, p. 161.

27. Worcester Cathedral Archives.

28. *Ibid.*

## 11. The Death of Studdert Kennedy, 1929

1. Worcester Cathedral Archives.

2. *Ibid.*

3. BBC Radio programme, 1962.

4. H. R. L. Sheppard, "Studdert Kennedy: A Friend", in J. K. Mozley (ed.), *G. A. Studdert Kennedy by his Friends*, London, Hodder & Stoughton, 1929, p. 201.

5. Interview with Andrew Studdert-Kennedy.

6. Michael Grundy, *A Fiery Glow in the Darkness: Woodbine Willie, Padre and Poet*, Worcester, Osborne Books, 1997, p. 81.

7. *Ibid.*, pp. 81–82.

8. William Purcell, *Woodbine Willie. A Study of Geoffrey Studdert*

*Kennedy*, London and Oxford, Mowbray Religious Reprints, 1982 (first published 1962), p. 214.

9. *Ibid.*, p. 215.

10. Worcester Cathedral Archives.

11. Grundy, *A Fiery Glow in the Darkness*, p. 81.

12. Worcester Cathedral Archives.

13. *Ibid.*

14. *Ibid.*

15. *Ibid.*

16. *Ibid.*

17. *Ibid.*

18. *Ibid.*

19. *Ibid.*

20. *Ibid.*

21. *Ibid.*

22. *Ibid.*

23. *Ibid.*

24. William Temple, "Studdert Kennedy The Man and his Message", in J. K. Mozley (ed.), *G. A. Studdert Kennedy by his Friends*, London, Hodder & Stoughton, 1929, p. 210.

25. *Ibid.*, pp. 218–19.

26. Worcester Cathedral Archives.

27. *Ibid.*

28. Temple, "Studdert Kennedy: The Man and his Message", p. 208.

29. Worcester Cathedral Archives.

30. *Ibid.*

31. *Ibid.*

32. *Ibid.*

33. *Ibid.*

34. *Ibid.*

35. *Ibid.*

36. *Ibid.*

37. *Ibid.*

38. *Ibid.*

39. *Ibid.*

40. *Ibid.*

41. *Ibid.*

42. Geoffrey A. Studdert Kennedy, *The New Man in Christ*, London, Hodder & Stoughton, 1932, p. 12.

43. *Ibid.*, p. 30.

44. *Ibid.*, p. 148.

45. *Ibid.*, p. 149.

46. *Ibid.*, pp. 251–52.

## 12. The Man, His Message and His Methods

1. William Purcell, *Woodbine Willie: A Study of Geoffrey Studdert Kennedy*, London and Oxford, Mowbray Religious Reprints, 1982 (first published 1962), pp. 20–21.

2. P. T. R. Kirk, "Studdert Kennedy: I. C. F. Crusader", in J. K. Mozley (ed.), *G. A. Studdert Kennedy by his Friends*, London, Hodder & Stoughton, 1929, p. 188.

3. Geoffrey A. Studdert Kennedy, *The New Man in Christ*, London, Hodder & Stoughton, 1932, p. 236.

4. Michael Grundy, *A Fiery Glow in the Darkness: Woodbine Willie, Padre and Poet*, Worcester, Osborne Books, 1997, p. 8.

5. Purcell, *Woodbine Willie*, p. 110.

6. Worcester Cathedral Archives.

7. Geoffrey A. Studdert Kennedy, *The Word and the Work*, London, Longmans, Green and Co., 1925, p. 39.

8. Worcester Cathedral Archives.

9. Purcell, *Woodbine Willie*, p. 110.

10. *Ibid.*, p. 15.

11. *Ibid.*, p. 16.

12. Kerry Walters (ed.), *After War, Is Faith Possible? G. A Studdert Kennedy "Woodbine Willie." An Anthology*, Cambridge, The Lutterworth Press, 2008, p. xi.

13. Paul Tongue, *Father Geoffrey Studdert Kennedy: Parish Priest*,

*Woodbine Willie. A Short Introduction* (pamphlet), Worcester, Worcester Cathedral, 2009, p. 6.

14. Interview with Andrew Studdert-Kennedy.

15. *Ibid.*

16. *Ibid.*

17. Studdert Kennedy, *The New Man in Christ*, p. 252.

18. Interview with Andrew Studdert-Kennedy.

19. *Ibid.*

20. BBC Radio programme, 1962.

21. *Ibid.*

22. Grundy, *A Fiery Glow in the Darkness*, p. 86.

23. *Ibid.*, p. 86.

24. Personal communication with Michael Studdert-Kennedy.

25. Grundy, *A Fiery Glow in the Darkness*, p. 86.

26. Interview with Andrew Studdert-Kennedy.

27. *Ibid.*

28. *Ibid.*

29. *Ibid.*

30. Personal communication with Michael Studdert-Kennedy.

31. *Ibid.*

32. Interview with Andrew Studdert-Kennedy.

33. *Ibid.*

34. H. R. L. Sheppard, "Studdert Kennedy: A Friend", in J. K. Mozley (ed.), *G. A. Studdert Kennedy by his Friends*, p. 199.

35. William Temple, "Studdert Kennedy: The Man and His Message", in J. K. Mozley (ed.), *G. A. Studdert Kennedy by his Friends*, p. 209.

36. Interview with Andrew Studdert-Kennedy.

37. Purcell, *Woodbine Willie*, p. 199.

38. *Ibid.*, p. 86.

39. BBC Radio programme, 1962.

40. Fenner Brockway, *Bermondsey Story: The Life of Alfred Salter*, London, Stephen Humphrey, 1995, p. 89.

41. D. F. Carey, "Studdert Kennedy: War Padre", in J. K. Mozley (ed.), *G. A. Studdert Kennedy by his Friends*, pp. 139–41.

42. *Ibid.*, p. 138.

43. Worcester Cathedral Archives.

44. Geoffrey A. Studdert Kennedy, *The Wicket Gate*, London, Hodder & Stoughton, 1923, p. 211.

45. BBC Radio programme, 1962.

46. *Ibid.*

47. *Ibid.*

48. *Ibid.*

49. Worcester Cathedral Archives.

50. *Ibid.*

51. BBC Radio programme, 1962.

52. Grundy, *A Fiery Glow in the Darkness*, p. 8.

53. Kenneth Woollcombe, "A Fiery Glow in the Darkness: The Influence of Studdert Kennedy on the Thinking of the Church" (public lecture), Worcester, Worcester Cathedral, 1999, p. 6.

54. Walters, *After War, Is Faith Possible?*, p. xi.

55. Bob Holman, *F. B. Meyer: If I Had a Hundred Lives*, Fearn, Christian Focus, 2007.

56. Purcell, *Woodbine Willie*, p. 178.

57. Grundy, *A Fiery Glow in the Darkness*, p. 73.

58. Timothy Heaton, *The Naturalist and the Christ*, Winchester, Circle Books, 2011, p. 103.

59. Walters, *After War, Is Faith Possible?*, p. 12.

60. Purcell, *Woodbine Willie*, p. 219.

61. Geoffrey A. Studdert Kennedy, *Food for the Fed-Up*, London, Hodder & Stoughton, 1921, p. 113.

62. *Ibid.*, p. 114.

63. Worcester Cathedral Archives.

64. Temple, "Studdert Kennedy: The Man And His Message", p. 211.

65. Studdert Kennedy, *Food for the Fed-Up*, pp. 110–11.

66. Studdert Kennedy, *The New Man in Christ*, p. 229.

67. Purcell, *Woodbine Willie*, p. 220.

68. Studdert Kennedy, *The New Man in Christ*, p. 224.

69. Kirk, "Studdert Kennedy. I. C. F. Crusader", p. 173.

70. Temple, "Studdert Kennedy: The Man and His Message", pp. 213–14.

71. A. J. P. Taylor, *English History 1914–1945*, London, Pelican Books, reprinted, 1987, p. 222.

72. Purcell, *Woodbine Willie*, pp. 206–207.

73. Studdert Kennedy, *The New Man in Christ*, p. 213.

74. Kirk, "Studdert Kennedy: I. C. F. Crusader", p. 168.

75. Alan Wilkinson, *The Church of England and the First World War*, London, SPCK, 1978, p. 90.

76. Frank Field, *Saints and Heroes: Inspiring Politics*, London, SPCK, 2010, p. 5.

77. William Temple, *The Hope of a New World*, London, Student Christian Movement Press, 1940 and *Christianity and Social Order*, Harmondsworth, Penguin, 1942.

78. Field, *Saints and Heroes*, p. 58.

79. Purcell, *Woodbine Willie*, p. 223.

80. Woollcombe, "A Fiery Glow in the Darkness", p. 6.

81. Neal Goldsborough, *Where is God Amidst the Bombs?* Cincinnati, OH, Forward Movement, 2008, p. 22.

82. *Ibid.*, p. 31.

83. *Ibid.*, p. 61.

84. *Ibid.*, p. 87.

85. Rowan Williams, "A Sermon at a Service to Mark the Passing of the World War One Generation", Westminster Abbey, 11 November 2009, p. 1; available online at http://www.archbishopofcanterbury.org/articles.php/857/a-sermon-at-a-service-to-mark-the-passing-of-the-world-war-one-generation.

86. *Ibid.*, p. 3.

87. *Ibid.*, p. 4.

88. Heaton, *The Naturalist and the Christ*, p. 75.

89. *Ibid.*, p. 116.

90. Personal communication with Nigel Studdert-Kennedy.

# Epilogue

1. Letter from Child Poverty Action Group, 25 November 2011.

2. Heather Stewart, "Working for Nothing", *The Observer*, 20 October 2011.

3. Katie Allen and James Ball, "Sharp fall in real earnings as pay gap widens", *The Guardian*, 24 November 2011.

4. Michael Meacher, letter to *The Guardian*, 24 January 2012.

5. Richard Wilkinson and Kate Pickett, *The Spirit Level: Why More Equal Societies Almost Always Do Better*, London, Allen Lane, 2009, chapters 4–12.

6. Bob Holman, *Keir Hardie: Labour's Greatest Hero?* Oxford, Lion Hudson, 2010, p. 151.

7. Andrew Rawnsley, *The End of the Party: The Rise and Fall of New Labour*, London, Penguin Books, 2010, p. 126.

8. *Speaker's Conference on Parliamentary Representation: Final Report*, London, House of Commons, 2010, p.19.

9. Felicity Lawrence, "Hunger is being used to spur the idle to work", *The Guardian*, 27 January 2012.

10. Reported in *Poverty*, November 2011, p. 4.

11. P. T. R. Kirk, "Studdert Kennedy: I. C. F. Crusader", in J. K. Mozley (ed.), *G. A. Studdert Kennedy By His Friends*, London, Hodder & Stoughton, 1929, p. 168.

12. Interview with Andrew Studdert-Kennedy.

# Bibliography

Brockway, Fenner, *Bermondsey Story: The Life of Alfred Salter*, London, Stephen Humphrey, 1995.

Brophy, John and Partridge, Eric (eds), *The Daily Telegraph Dictionaries of Tommies' Songs and Slang 1914–18*, London, Frontline Books, 2008.

Brown, Malcolm, "After Ninety Years", in John Brophy and Eric Partridge (eds), *The Daily Telegraph Dictionaries of Tommies' Songs and Slang 1914–18*, London, Frontline Books, 2008.

Dale, Graham, *God's Politicians*, London, HarperCollins, 2000.

Ensor, Sir Robert, *England 1870–1914*, Oxford, Clarendon Press, reprinted 1966.

Field, Frank, *Saints and Heroes: Inspiring Politics*, London, SPCK, 2010.

Fiennes, Peter, *To War With God: The Army Chaplain Who Lost His Faith*, Edinburgh and London, SPCK, 2010.

Gazeley, Iain and Newell, Andrew, *Poverty in Britain in 1904*, Brighton, University of Sussex, 2007.

Goldsborough, Neal, *Where is God Amidst the Bombs?* Cincinnati, OH, Forward Movement, 2008.

Grundy, Michael, *A Fiery Glow in the Darkness: Woodbine Willie, Padre and Poet*, Worcester, Osborne Books, 1997.

Hanbury-Sparrow, Alan, "Front Line Chaplain", in Kenneth Brill (ed.), *John Groser: East End Priest*, London and Oxford, Mowbrays, 1971.

Hankey, Donald, *A Student in Arms*, London, Alan Melrose Ltd, 1918.

Hart, Christopher, *The History and Architecture of St Paul's Church, Worcester* (pamphlet), Worcester, St Paul's Church, 1995.

Heaton, Timothy, *The Naturalist and the Christ*, Winchester, Circle Books, 2011.

Holman, Bob, *Good Old George: The Life of George Lansbury*, Oxford, Lion, 1990.

— —, *F. B. Meyer: If I had a Hundred Lives*, Fearn, Christian Focus, 2007.

— —, *Keir Hardie: Labour's Greatest Hero?* Oxford, Lion Hudson, 2010.

Johnson, J. H., *Stalemate! The Real Story of Trench Warfare*, London, Rigel Publications, 1995.

Kirk, P. T. R., "Studdert Kennedy: I C. F. Crusader", in J. K. Mozley (ed.), *G. A. Studdert Kennedy by his Friends*, London, Hodder & Stoughton, 1929.

Lansbury, George, *Your Part in Poverty*, London, Allen and Unwin, 1917.

Lowe, Norman, *Mastering Modern British History*, London, Macmillan, 2nd edition, 1989.

Montague, C. E., *Disenchantment*, London, Chatto and Windus, 1922.

Moore Ede, William, "His Life in Worcester", in Mozley, J. K. (ed.), *G. A. Studdert Kennedy by his Friends*, London, Hodder & Stoughton, 1929.

Mozley, J. K. (ed.), *G. A. Studdert Kennedy by his Friends,* London, Hodder & Stoughton, 1929.

Mozley, J. K., "Home Life and Early Years of Ministry", in J. K. Mozley (ed.), *G. A. Studdert Kennedy by his Friends*, London, Hodder & Stoughton, 1929.

Mozley, J. K., "Epilogue", in J. K. Mozley (ed.), *G. A. Studdert Kennedy by his Friends*, London, Hodder & Stoughton, 1929.

Overy, Richard, *The Morbid Age*, London, Penguin Books, 2010.

Purcell, William, *Woodbine Willie: A Study of Geoffrey Studdert Kennedy*, London and Oxford, Mowbray Religious Reprints (first published 1962), 1982.

Rawnsley, Andrew, *The End of the Party: The Rise and Fall of New Labour*, London, Penguin Books, 2010.

Rowntree, Benjamin Seebohm, *A Study of Town Life*, London, Macmillan, 1901.

Sheffield, Gary, *The First World War: The Road to War* (pamphlet), London, *The Guardian*, 2008.

Sheppard, H. R. L., "Studdert Kennedy: A Friend", in J. K. Mozley (ed.), *G. A. Studdert Kennedy by his Friends*, London, Hodder & Stoughton, 1929.

*Speaker's Conference on Parliamentary Representation: Final Report*, London, House of Commons, 2010.

Studdert Kennedy, Geoffrey A., *Rough Rhymes of a Padre*, London, Hodder & Stoughton, 1918.

— —, *Rough Talks by a Padre*, London, Hodder & Stoughton, 1918.

— —, *The Hardest Part*, London, Hodder & Stoughton, 1918.

— —, *Lies*, London, Hodder & Stoughton, 1919.

— —, *Democracy and the Dog Collar*, London, Hodder & Stoughton, 1921.

— —, *Food for the Fed-Up*, London, Hodder & Stoughton, 1921.

— —, *The Wicket Gate,* London, Hodder & Stoughton, 1923.

— —, *The Word and the Work*, London, Longmans, Green and Co., 1925.

— —, *I Pronounce Them: The Story of Man and Wife, London*, Hodder & Stoughton, 1927.

— —, *The Unutterable Beauty,* London, Hodder & Stoughton, 1927. Reprinted as *The Rhymes of G. A. Studdert Kennedy*, London, Hodder & Stoughton, 1940.

— —, *The Warrior, the Woman and the Christ*, London, Hodder & Stoughton, 1928.

— —, *The New Man in Christ*, London, Hodder & Stoughton, 1932.

Studdert-Kennedy, Gerald, *Dog-Collar Democracy: The Industrial Christian Fellowship 1919–1929*, London, Macmillan Press, 1982.

Studdert Kennedy, Hugh, *The Visitor*, London, Putnam & Co. Ltd, 1934.

Tawney, Richard, *The Attack and Other Papers*, Nottingham, Spokesman, 1981.

Taylor, A. J. P., *English History 1914–1945*, London, Pelican Books, reprinted 1987.

Temple, "Studdert Kennedy: The Man and his Message", in J. K. Mozley (ed.), *G. A. Studdert Kennedy by his Friends*, London, Hodder & Stoughton, 1929.

— —, *The Hope of a New World*, London, Student Christian Movement Press, 1940.

— —, William, *Christianity and Social Order*, Harmondsworth, Penguin, 1942.

Terrill, Ross, *R. H. Tawney and His Times*, London, Andre Deutsch, 1974.

Thomson, David, *England in the Twentieth Century 1914–1963*, London, Harmondsworth, Penguin Books, reprinted 1978.

Tongue, Paul, *Father Geoffrey Studdert Kennedy, Parish Priest, Woodbine Willie: A Short Introduction* (pamphlet), Worcester, Worcester Cathedral, 2009.

Walsh, Michael (ed.), *Dictionary of Christian Biography*, London and New York, Continuum Press, 2001.

Walters, Kerry (ed.), *After War, is Faith Possible? G. A. Studdert Kennedy "Woodbine Willie": An Anthology*, Cambridge, The Lutterworth Press, 2008.

Wilkinson, Alan, *The Church of England and the First World War*, London, SPCK, 1978.

Wilkinson, Alan, *Dissent or Conform? War, Peace and the English Churches 1900–1945*, London, SCM Press, 1986.

Wilkinson, Richard and Pickett, Kate, *The Spirit Level. Why More Equal Societies Almost Always Do Better*, London, Allen Lane, 2009.

Williams, Rowan, "A Sermon at a Service to Mark the Passing of the World War One Generation", Westminster Abbey, 11 November 2009; available online at http://www.archbishopofcanterbury.org/articles. php/857/a-sermon-at-a-service-to-mark-the-passing-of-the-world-war-one-generation.

Woollcombe, Kenneth, "A Fiery Glow in the Darkness: The Influence of Studdert Kennedy on the Thinking of the Church" (public lecture), Worcester, Worcester Cathedral, 1997.

*Note.* Studdert Kennedy published a number of books of poems. All of his poems used in this book, except one, are taken from his *The Unutterable Beauty*, London, Hodder & Stoughton, 1927. The exception is the original form of "A Sermon in a Billet" which is found in D. F. Carey, "Studdert Kennedy: War Padre", in J. K. Mozley (ed.), *G. A. Studdert Kennedy by His Friends*, London, Hodder & Stoughton, 1929, pp. 133–35.

# INDEX